BOY IN THE CORNER

Clyde D. Batavia

www.Lrpnv.com

Published in the United States of America by LeRue Books an imprint
of LeRue Press, LLC.

Printed in the United States of America by LeRue Press (LRP). No part
of this book may be used or reproduced, in any manner, performed or
copied in any form without written permission except in the case of
brief quotations embodied in critical articles and reviews.

The author attempted to recreate events, locales and conversations as
accurately as possible. In order to maintain anonymity, in some
instances, he has changed some identifying characteristics and details
such as physical properties, occupations and places of residence.

For permission to reprint contact: LeRue Press, LLC, 280 Greg Street,
#10, Reno, Nevada 89502
inquiry@Leruepress.com

www.Leruepress.com

Cover photo: Getty Image Credit, Holloway
Author photo: Jeff Batavia

ISBN: 978-1-938814-35-8
First Edition, 2021

Library of Congress Control Number: 2021911198

10 9 8 7 6 5 4 3 2 1

DEDICATION

*Dedicated to my mother who never let me
quit anything I tried, and Patty Marshall
Monson who kept at me to write the book.
Special thanks to Patricia Swanson
who spent hours proof reading. .*

PREFACE

My motivation for writing this book is to hopefully help children with learning difficulties. It has taken me seventy-four years to realize I am not a dummy. Even though the scar that I received in a time before they knew what learning disabilities were. You will come to see that even though I never possessed the skills to read, write and spell properly I managed to accomplish many things.

Some of my goals were quite complex yet due to determination it was achievable. I want those who struggle with academics to realize they can achieve anything they put their minds and efforts towards. There is always an alternate way to reach ones goal. The trick is in finding a way to get what you want.

You will see that when it comes to education there is no one size that fits everyone. As my son who is a principal of a school tells me, it is easy to teach smart kids. It takes a good teacher to teach to those who are having learning issues. I hope you will find this book inspiring and motivating.

TABLE OF CONTENTS

CHAPTER I
OFF TO SCHOOL

The summer of 1950 was my last summer vacation before the start of my formal education, or so I thought. There were six of us kids living in the same neighborhood: Patty, Eddie, Gary, Don, Tommy and me. We were the same age, and we played together almost every day and into the evening until the sound of our moms called us home. The six of us have remained friends into adulthood. Unfortunately, we lost Eddie first, and then Patty, who died suddenly in 2018. I still see or talk on the phone with Gary and Tommy, although Tommy moved east and I haven't heard from him in a long time. Don and I have remained best friends, and we talk at least once a week. We all took advantage of playing every day, knowing that we would be starting kindergarten in the fall. Redwood Heights Grammar School was situated across the street from Patty's, Don's and my house. Eddie, Gary and Tommy lived just down the street. The school had a huge playground, and for years we rode our bicycles on it as if it were our own back yard.

We were excited about going to school together, which overcame our nervousness. The anticipation we all had from years of watching the kids going to and from the school was pure excitement. I guess we all thought we would be in the same class together.

1950 was the best summer yet, and it passed very quickly. Patty was the only girl in our group; the rest of us were boys. When we played cowboys and Indians, which was big for that time period, Patty had a Dale Evans' outfit, while us guys were outfitted as Roy Rogers, or Hop -a-long Cassidy. Part of the ritual of starting school was everyone going shopping with their moms to get their new back to school clothes.

Our parents all moved into the Redwood Heights neighborhood of Oakland about the same time. All of us kids were about the same age of three. It was a very friendly environment, and during the summer it was common to have neighborhood parties. Our parents became friends, as this was post World War II era, and almost all the fathers had served in the military. There was a definite bond among the neighbors. Our gang of six was inseparable. We were more like brothers and sister. We did everything together, and when one of us needed watching, it was common for one of the other parents to take care of us.

Then came word from the Oakland Board of Education that those whose birthdays fell in August or later would not be attending kindergarten in September. The school board was implementing a new change which they called mid-semesters. The theory was to give the younger kids more time to mature.

Because my birthday was in October I would be left behind along with Tommy. You can only imagine how devastated I was. I can remember to this day feeling how unfair the situation had become. I was angry with the school board. Thinking back, it put a nasty taste in my mouth for school before I even got there. I already didn't like what they had done to me, and I am guessing it influenced my negativity for education.

Tommy and I became closer, as we spent a lot time together waiting for our turn to go to school in January. Naturally, we thought we would be reunited and put in the same class with our friends. That couldn't have been further from the truth! In fact, all of us mid-semester kids were placed together in the same class. I am sure that didn't help my outlook on school. It just reinforced my dislike of it. I wanted to be with my friends and the kids I knew, but the mold had been cast, and my disappointment with school followed me the rest of my life. On top of all that, there were no tests to determine basic skills in students. Therefore, the school had no way of knowing that I had learning disabilities and dyslexia.

As the days slowly passed from September to January, I became a real irritant on Mom. There was really nothing to do, and Tommy wasn't always available to play. It seemed like time was going way too slowly. I missed all my friends. My mother said she couldn't wait for me to finally get out of her hair and start school.

When she had had enough of my attitude, she would yell from the kitchen: "I have had it with you Clyde. Go play on the freeway."

Mom's other favorite was, "Wait 'til your father gets home!"

Finally, January came, and Mom and I were both ready for me to go to kindergarten. Although, maybe Mom was more ready than I...

CHAPTER II
KINDERGARTEN TRAUMA

My first day of kindergarten was a huge disappointment. After what seemed an eternity, the day had finally arrived when I could be with my friends, only to find out the rest of the gang was in another classroom. What a disaster! Ah, but there was recess which immediately became my favorite part of education throughout my school years. Unfortunately, recess time was always way too short, and fifty minutes between recesses was too far apart for my liking. I guess I thought kindergarten was going to be like playing with my friends in the neighborhood.

Mrs. Thompson was my kindergarten teacher. She wasted no time in trying to create some kind of order and discipline within the classroom. I found myself being told that I had to raise my hand to be recognized before I could talk. Not only that but, I couldn't leave my seat without permission, and worst of all: I had to listen.

This seemed more like jail, not school. What happened to having fun? My world was being turned upside down, and I didn't like it. It felt very restrictive to me and I sensed that I had lost my freedom.

In the days and years to follow it became increasingly more difficult for me to progress in school.

The first restrictive issue that faced me was my size. I was one of the shortest in my class, and we were made to line up by height, short people in the front. Teachers seemed to use this height thing in school for everything: fire drills, air-raid drills, going out for recess, assemblies and especially where we sat in the classroom.

I was always right in front of the teacher. I was sure this was all a ploy to separate me from anyone I liked, even from Tommy, the only friend from our gang. To my disappointment I could not sit next to him. I didn't like what I was seeing and immediately questioned Mrs. Thompson. I was told not to speak without raising my hand.

So began my confrontational attitude with teachers. I didn't much care for Mrs. Thompson's attitude towards me and I realized this was not going to be as much fun as I had at first thought. In kindergarten we had tables instead of desks and the short people's table was placed toward the front of the classroom. In fact, until college, we short people were always stuck in the front of the classroom. This meant I was right under Mrs. Thompson's view!

Everything was changing around me faster than I could process. The person who was instrumental in these changes was Mrs. Thompson. I must have decided I was not going to let her get away with this and would show her who was in charge. One of first assignments was learning the pledge of allegiance to the flag. The pledge was recited every morning before class got under way. We were given a deadline to memorize it. Mrs. Thompson said she would call on someone each day to lead the pledge, so we'd better be prepared.

We also had to line up for fire drills and air raid drills. Air raid drills were very big in the fifties and early sixties. We were to line up by height and were told be quiet and listen for instructions. The best part of the fire drill was getting out of the classroom. We would march outside to the playground where I would see my friends all lined up like our class. I constantly got in trouble for talking to the other kids when I was supposed to be listening, or at least waiting for instructions.

The air-raid drills were conducted differently. We would line up by height and then we were all led out into the hallway and told to sit with our backs against the wall, knees up to our chest, and cover our heads in our knees. It was very uncomfortable for me, so I was constantly fidgeting around trying to get more comfortable. I would soon be reprimanded for fidgeting, and as soon as I would try and explain why I was fidgeting it only brought me more trouble. It didn't take long before I was labeled the class cutup! The other kids didn't seem to create problems for Mrs. Thompson, but I became the example for what not to do.

There were rewards for the good students. They could be the milk monitor, get to pass out the graham crackers for snacks, or be the ball monitor and get to be first to choose toys to play with in the classroom. I was always excluded from being chosen.

I loved recess, and "share and tell" was a big hit with me. My little hand would be raised up, waving all over the place. I would say, "Mrs. Thompson, Mrs. Thompson, me, me"! I thought Mrs. Thompson was just being mean when she would call on someone else.

She would say, "Clyde, you need to wait your turn!" and the other kids would laugh.

I really began to dislike her and began thinking how I would get even with her. Recess was becoming even more my most favorite thing in school, and it never came soon enough. My school days were beginning to be a war of wills: my will versus Mrs. Thompson's!

When the day came and I was finally called on to lead the Pledge of Allegiance, fear set in! I had not memorized it, and now I was going to have to stand in front of the flag, my hand over my heart, and lead the class in the pledge. I tried to bluff my way through it by making up words.

I got great laughs from the other kids, but Mrs. Thompson said, "Clyde, see that red chair in the corner of the cloak closet? Go and sit there and be quiet."

I believe that was the moment I became labeled the dummy of the class and the class clown. Both names followed me during my entire time in elementary school. It was also the last time I was called on to lead the Pledge of Allegiance.

Our classroom probably looked like most elementary schools of that era with linoleum floors, radiator heating, and a cloak room. The cloak room was a separate room but open in the front facing the classroom. It was where we put our lunch boxes, coats, rain boots, and raincoats. Not long after my educational career began, the cloak room became an intimate place for me to spend time. I spent many an hour sitting in the red chair in the corner looking at all the kids' stuff. As kindergarten dragged on, the only ray of hope was that spring would soon become summer, and school would be out, yea!

The summer brought me hope that things would be better at school the next fall. I thought for sure I would then be back with my neighborhood friends in the same class. No one would be left behind this time. I would have a new teacher and a clean slate. No way could things be as bad as what I had just suffered in kindergarten.

CHAPTER III
FRUSTRATION AND DISAPPOINTMENT

My balloon burst and my hopes were ripped apart on the first day of first grade. Those sneaky teachers over the summer had plotted against me again by deciding to create a lower first grade and regular first grade. Guess where most of us that started school as mid-termers were put? That's right. The majority of us ended up in the lower first grade.

In my mind, this was a plan designed against me personally! I remember feeling that hollow pit in my stomach and frustration and anger towards the teachers. I definitely was going to show them they couldn't mess with me! A line in the sand had been drawn! They wanted to keep me from being with the gang of six.

The teachers in the lower first grade made us feel that we were not as good as or as smart as those in the regular first grade. I was wondering how this could be since we were all the same age. We all played together, and I hadn't noticed any difference in ability among Eddie, Gary or me. Just because their birthdays were earlier, I didn't see how that should make them smarter. It was extremely painful to me and created a scar in my brain which has never left me to this day.

Mrs. McIntosh, who taught both lower first grade and lower second grade, was my first and second grade teacher. She was an older lady, or that was my perspective as a seven-year-old. She reminded me of several babysitters I had in the past. By now I had not only lost interest in school, I found it very difficult to excel. First grade is where we began to learn numbers and letters. We were also introduced to the book Dick, Jane, and Spot. Every day started the same with the Pledge of Allegiance.

In second grade we were assigned desks, which were in three rows, one behind the other. Once again, the shortest kids were assigned to the front rows. I was right under Mrs. McIntosh's view and remember thinking how unfair that was. I had the feeling that I was being picked on since Mrs. McIntosh could now keep an eye on me at all times.

The other kids seemed to grasp instructions easily and do things like making their numbers and letters correctly. They could also keep them within the lines on the paper. Then there was me. When everyone's work was collected, mine would have my letters or numbers outside of the lined borders. We were given a big piece of unfinished paper which looked like it had particles of wood in it. The paper had wide lines to help us practice making our letters inside the lines. We had to make the capitals before learning the small letters. I seemed to have a problem making them neat and within the lines.

What seemed a simple task for others was difficult for me. I became the class example of how not to make the letters. I didn't do much better when it came to making numbers. The teacher would ask me to bring my paper to the front of the class. She would show my work and tell the class this was not how it was to be done. I remember the easiest numbers for me to make were one, seven and ten.

It wasn't long before Mrs. McIntosh thought I was not performing well on purpose. Her criticism of me began to be a daily occurrence. I guess she felt embarrassing me in front of the class would motivate me to do better. It only made me feel worse. I wanted to be like the others, but for some reason I just couldn't do writing exercises the way Mrs. McIntosh wanted. When the bell rang at the end of the day, she would ask me to wait as the kids all filed out of the classroom.

She would say, "Are you just stupid, dumb, or retarded? All the other kids can do the work. What is wrong with you?"

I was constantly being made to feel I was stupid and a failure, and I began to believe it to be true. After all, everyone else seem to be able to do the work. Since Mrs. McIntosh thought I was dumb, I would show her she was right, that I was dumb and incapable of learning. I thought, hopefully, she would quit using me as a bad example and leave me alone. That cloak room became my shelter from having to learn. Unfortunately, at seven years old, I didn't realize how important these formative years would be throughout my life.

Before the class could advance to the next level of learning, which was how to read, we were taught to make our letters. Once we could make them, we would put them together to form words. At this time in Oakland, teachers were using a new method of teaching reading called "sight relationship". We were using index cards with a picture and word for the picture on the card. Unfortunately, most of my friends who were in this experiment also had problems with sounding out words.

For example, on the index card was a picture of a cat and the word "cat" under it. We had to memorize each word so that when we saw the word, we would know it was a cat. This new experiment failed miserably and several years later, teachers went back to teaching words phonetically.

We also had a spelling test every week. We would be given a list of 20 words to memorize. I had trouble memorizing them, so I would miss many words on the test. At this time, teachers were using flash cards instead of using phonetics.

After some time practicing with sight cards, we all received our first book. The book was <u>Dick, Jane and Spot</u>. If I hadn't had enough problems with numbers, letters, and learning vocabulary, now I was going to have to put this all together so I could read a sentence or two. The panic I felt was unbelievable. I was drowning, falling farther and farther behind the other students. I could feel disaster brewing within me.

I hadn't found much to like about school so far, and now I failed miserably at having to read when called on. I struggled putting words together because I was slow processing them. It was hard enough trying to read. When the bell for recess came and we went outside to play, I can remember being called "stupid" by the some of the other students. The girls were never as mean as the boys.

To this day reading is very difficult for me and I do everything I can to avoid it. To me it's like taking someone who has a hard time playing golf and making them play every day. I must have thought if I couldn't compete with the others in reading, I certainly had a talent for making the kids laugh. Looking back, it was an outlet for me to gain acceptance and attention from the other kids. My making up words and pretending to read what wasn't really in the book got great laughter from the class. It also landed me in the corner of the cloak closet on a small red chair facing the jackets. So many trips to the cloak room also brought my mom's wrath in her meetings with the teachers. What was to be done with Clyde? How could the teachers get him to engage with the program?

In the fifties there was no such thing as learning centers, and no one was tuned into what we call today "special needs kids" or kids with learning disabilities. You were just labeled a behavior problem.

Patty, Eddie, Don, Clyde, 1949

It wasn't that I didn't want to achieve like the others; in fact, I wanted more than anything to be normal and fit in. I used to think how great it would be to come home with good report cards. It just wasn't happening during my formative years.

It wasn't long after this that Mrs. McIntosh seldom called on me. The only way left for me to get any attention was by acting up, which always ended up the same: me in the red chair in the corner of the cloak room. Meanwhile my education was suffering as I was not learning basic skills.

Back-to-school night brought more misery—this time, from my parents when they got home. There were no pictures on the classroom wall by Clyde and the teachers didn't have many positive things to say except "Clyde needs to improve on his work ethic and citizenship. I couldn't wait for first grade to be over, so I would get a clean slate in second grade. The shock of shocks was that Mrs. McIntosh was going to be my second grade teacher. What did I do to deserve this? There was no escaping from the humiliation I felt.

Years later, I would learn how I got Mrs. McIntosh for second grade. My father, who was a graduate of the University of California, took our family to the Lair of the Bear family camp in Pinecrest, California during the summers of 1951 to 1962. It was run by the University of California. My wife had also attended the same camp with her parents. I knew some day when I had a family, I would treat them to the experiences I had so enjoyed. Years later and married with a family of my own, we decided to go to the Lair for our family vacation. Everyone slept in tents with wooden sides and canvas tops. We slept in sleeping bags on wire mesh cots. Each tent had one light bulb in the middle of the ceiling. Camp staffers were university students. The dining hall was an open building with a roof and long rows of tables like picnic tables. A large metal triangle would be rung before meals. It could be heard all over the camp, and everyone would head to the dining hall. There was no assigned seating, so you never knew who else might be sitting at the table where you were sitting. At the time I was in my thirties and sitting at a table with my family. A lady who looked older than me was sitting across from me and kept staring at me.

She finally said, "Excuse me. Are you Clyde?"

I had no idea who she was. I answered, "Yes I am."

She said, "I was a teacher at Redwood Heights School, and I can remember that we use to flip a coin to see who was going to have you in their class the next year."

I finally had the answer about how I ended up with Mrs. McIntosh for second grade. I can't even begin to tell you the wound it reopened in me. It was like I could never escape from those early years.

CHAPTER IV

TESTING

I believe it was third grade where everyone took the Stanford-Binet standardized test given throughout the State of California. This test was to measure the students' cognitive ability in five areas: reasoning, knowledge, quantitative reasoning, visual process, and working memory. We sat at our desks and were given booklets, which we were told not to open until instructed to do so. Soft lead pencils were passed out. We were told to put them in the slot on the top of the desk designed for pencils. We were not to touch the pencil until instructed to do so.

On the front of the cover, we were to put our name by filling in small slots using the alphabetical letter above each small slot. As I recall, each test was timed. The questions were all multiple choice. The verbal instructions were given by our teacher who told us when we could start. We were to pick up our pencil and fill the slots that corresponded to our name and then open the booklet and begin the test. By the time I had figured out how to enter my name using the little slots, I could see most of my classmates were well on their way with the test.

I did not do well. When we were told there were five minutes left to go, I just filled in those little slots so that I would finish. I didn't even guess at the answers. My recollection is that I was not supposed to guess, and only answer the questions I knew the answers to. I didn't do well on the IQ testing either. I guess these are some of the reasons why I was constantly being told I would never succeed in life.

I had pretty much the same experience with different teachers in elementary school. There were some I liked better than others. For the fourth and fifth grades, I had Mr. Graft. I liked him because he was much more patient and took an interest in helping me succeed. I was still way behind the class in studies, but with Mr. Graft at least I wasn't getting N's. For those of you who don't know in the 1950's grades were E=excellent, G= good, S=satisfactory, N= needs improvement, and U= unsatisfactory. Thanks to Mr. Graft, in the subject matter area I was now getting mostly S's. My citizenship grades, due to a lack of my self-control, seemed to always be letter N. It didn't seem to matter how hard I tried I just couldn't seem to get my citizenship grade in the S range.

No matter what happened in class negatively, I would be the number one suspect on the teacher's list. I can't remember how many times I got called out for talking when I was innocent. Our desks were set up in vertical rows. The person behind me would tap me on the shoulder, and when I would turn around to see what that person wanted, I would get called out for talking. The minute I tried to explain myself, I only got more grief from the teacher. Note passing during class was common. When someone wanted to pass a note to someone, you would get a tap on the shoulder and the person behind you would ask that you pass it up to the next person. I would turn to take the note to pass it on and typically get caught. The teacher would think it must be me, since I was considered a behavioral problem. Once labeled, it always followed me through the school system.

Kids in grammar school in the fifties enjoyed many field trips and activities. The ones who had good citizenship marks were chosen to be the milk monitor, erase the chalk board, choose teams, and go to the circus, opera, or plays. More than anything I really wanted to be on traffic squad. Many of my friends were on it. They got to wear a red jacket and yellow hat. Some were officers, and they marched the others in formation to the different cross walks carrying the traffic signs with the big red octagonal letters that said "STOP".

Once again, I was left out of these activities due to my citizenship grades. I would be sent to the class below mine on that day or I would be sent to the principal's office to spend the day. When the others in my class came back from the circus, opera, milk farm, and many other excursions, it was hard for me to listen to them talk and share the experience they had just had.

When they were asked to write a paper reviewing their trip, I was left out again. I don't remember ever going on a field trip during my grammar school years. Instead, I was made to feel different and an outcast. It went right along with being told I would never succeed in life. These teachers were doing all they could to support their belief of my ineptitude. Looking back, I realize there was no consideration for my well-being. The scar that was being embossed in my brain was be-coming irreversible.

I was excluded from going with the rest of my class on field trips, I was constantly hearing from my teachers that I wouldn't amount to anything, and my mom was spending a large amount of time meeting with my teachers. I began to believe I couldn't succeed. My mom was a rock and would not accept the teachers' and school's evaluation that I was not smart and would never amount to anything. She took the educators to task. She was relentless in making them teach me. She was also relentless on me!

Mom was constantly making sure I was doing modified assignments, since I wasn't able to keep up with the rest of my class. Whatever the experts in education suggested, Mom would try. There was a period of time when I was taken out of class in the afternoon twice a week. It had been explained to me that my mom was taking me to a learning center for extra help, which sounded okay to me. I had not reflected on this until the writing of this book. Now I realize that the person I saw was either a child psychologist or perhaps a psychiatrist.

I enjoyed these sessions as I was away from school. I would be asked what or who I didn't like in school, such as a particular teacher or perhaps a student. Then I would be asked to draw a picture of whoever I had said I didn't like. The picture would be put on a cork board held by a thumb tack. I would be handed three darts, and told it was okay to throw them at my picture. Then I would be asked if it made me feel better. Thinking back now, I am surprised I didn't become a serial killer. As I am writing this 68 years later, I am pretty sure the place I went to wasn't a learning center, but I guess they were trying to figure out what made me tick.

CHAPTER V
PILING ON

My family being of the Jewish faith, belonged to Temple Sinai in Oakland. Jewish children were expected to attend Sunday school, and at age 13 it was a custom for boys to have a Bar Mitzvah. That entailed learning Hebrew and reciting prayers in Hebrew and English in front of the congregation. Like public schools, Temple Sinai ran a structured Sunday school. It went from kindergarten through tenth grade. At the end of tenth grade, we went through confirmation. Once confirmed, we were done with any more formal Jewish education.

If regular school wasn't enough for me to handle, I now had to attend Sunday school, which ran way too many hours on Sunday. My perspective at this time was that my free time was being eaten up with schools! If these things weren't bad enough already, I now had homework to do from both. I might as well have had my fingernails pulled out with pliers.

Two years before my Bar Mitzvah, I started Hebrew school. The count was now three schools I had to attend. Hebrew school the first year was only once a week on a Tuesday after school. It ran from four in the afternoon till five in the evening.

The year before my Bar Mitzvah I had to go twice a week. The only saving grace was that my parents didn't put the emphasis on my grades as seriously as my public school teachers did. They were just happy I was going without a fight. When I look back at my Sunday school report cards, they were pretty much identical to my public school report cards.

"Clyde has trouble staying focused and pays little attention", or "Clyde is constantly disrupting the class."

My behavior pattern was not much different in Sunday school than public school. Here I was disliking school, and my parents kept adding more for me to attend and deal with. In looking back, in the 1950's, little was known about ADHD and learning disabilities.

One size teaching fit everyone. If you marched to a different tune or learned differently, the teachers looked for the easiest way to deal with you as the problem student. Therefore, I was classified as a discipline problem early on, which followed me all through school. By not working with me or giving me special consideration, I was cheated out of those formative years of learning the basic skills I needed to advance.

During my fifth-grade year, my parents were building a new house in the Oakland Hills. I was informed that I would be changing schools and doing my last year of grammar school at a new school. I liked my friends where I was and had known them all before school ever began. I had never had a problem with being socially accepted, and I had many friends, who accepted me regardless of my lack of academic achievements. The thought of going to a new school and having to make new friends was very upsetting and stressful to me, and once again I found myself being separated from the gang of 6.

And once again I was going to be the "different one" in a new school environment.

As they say when one door closes another one opens. Once I accepted the idea that our family was going to move and I would be attending a new school, I surrendered. I must have realized that I'd better make the best of it. During the summer of 1957 we moved into our new home, and it wasn't long before I met a few of the guys in the neighborhood. I realized they knew nothing about me or my reputation that had followed me from my old school. I thought this could be good as at that point I had a clean slate with no negative label associated with me. It was time to turn over a new leaf. The stigma of not being very smart was not what I wanted people to think about me.

CHAPTER VI
BAR MITZVAH

Summer came and went, and September meant time to start at the new school. I also had matured a little more. Sixth grade here I go! I was put in Mrs. Walden's class. I thought to myself: "Don't act out and keep your mouth shut". So I did. My citizenship grades for the first time in my school career were good. Not only did this please my parents, but home life was becoming easier for me. Unfortunately, on the academic side I didn't have the foundation I needed to excel or even stay in the middle of the curve.

When I had been told from the beginning about the importance of learning the basics of reading, writing and arithmetic; I either didn't want to accept, didn't understand, or was incapable of learning. It is hard to explain to someone who for the first 5 years of school spent most of his time sitting in the corner of the cloak room on that little red chair facing the hanging jackets.

Fighting the school system along the way cost me valuable time. Besides, I obviously didn't learn like most kids. Trying to make up for all the lost time was impossible. It didn't take me long to realize this new concept, and I could see and feel that this was going to be a difficult feat. I was one of youngest in my class and never had the maturity to realize that going from one

Clyde D. Batavia

grade to the next meant building on the basic skills learned at the beginning.

Because my basic skill level was very weak at best, I now found myself struggling to maintain the same level of learning as the other students, although at my new school I had no prior bad reputation and was getting good citizenship grades. I actually managed to get through the sixth grade with average grades and a good reputation.

Also, during sixth grade I was studying for my Bar Mitzvah, which would occur on my thirteenth birthday in October. In the Jewish religion a boy becomes a man when he completes his Bar Mitzvah. The process entails a fair amount of studying Hebrew, writing a speech and learning all the prayers in Hebrew.

On the day of the Bar Mitzvah I had to conduct the entire service. There were probably over 200 people present. Then when the service was over, a party followed, as was the custom, to celebrate my becoming a man. This was a big deal and was also very important to my parents and grandparents.

Once again, I needed a tutor to help me with learning Hebrew and writing my speech. The learning required took a lot of discipline. I could hardly understand English, let alone knowing that I had to learn Hebrew. Somehow, though, with tutors and many Saturdays spent going over and over the material, I managed to accomplish my goal and have my Bar Mitzvah.

I don't know who was more surprised, me or my family and friends! I had actually done a great job, just like my friends had at their Bar Mitzvahs. I had invited friends from both Sunday school and public school. My old friends were very impressed with my performance, whereas my new friends didn't know about my learning issues. Many had never been to a Bar Mitzvah, so it was a new experience for them.

I was now being seen in a different light. I was no longer being called a dummy or being embarrassed by a teacher in front of a class. I certainly was feeling better about myself. I think I was realizing I could accomplish things. I liked that I was being accepted by my peers and being treated like everyone else. I was no longer the clown or class cut up.

Years later Patty started pushing me into writing a story about my education: this one. She had been on the Oakland School Board and had a deep feeling that all children should be able to get a good education. It has taken me these 68 years to accomplish that task.

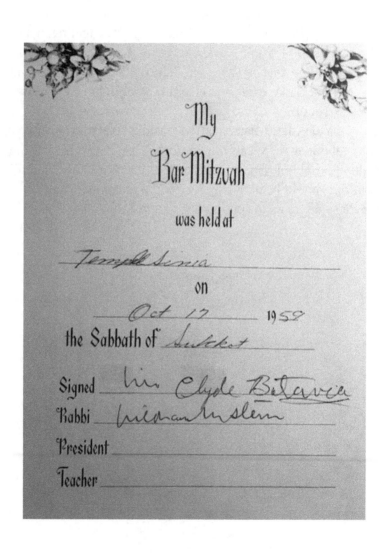

My
Bar Mitzvah

was held at

Temple Sinai

on

Oct 17 1959

the Sabbath of Sukkot

Signed _____ Clyde Batavia

Rabbi _____ Michael Mislen

President _____

Teacher _____

CHAPTER VII
CHANGING SCHOOLS

A new junior high school was built up the hill, about 100 yards from my grammar school. The first half of the year we were stuck in portable buildings that were used until the completion of Montera Junior High. It opened after Christmas break.

The student body was comprised of kids from several grammar schools in the surrounding area and was like being in a large mixing bowl. Junior high was very different for all of us. We moved from classroom to classroom every fifty minutes. There was no recess, only those few minutes to get to the next class. Instead of recess every fifty minutes we now had an entire fifty minutes devoted to gym class. In those days it was mandatory for the boys and girls to change into gym clothes. The boys' locker room had showers and everyone showered together in one large area. The towel monitor would hand out clean towels every day. Also new to us in junior high was the variety of classes we could take. Once a month on Friday afternoons there would be sock hops (dances) in the cafeteria/auditorium.

I found the format of junior high much more to my liking than grammar school. I was no longer stuck with the same teacher for the entire day. Although it was a better fit for me, I found no matter how hard I tried, my classes never got any easier.

My parents arranged for tutors, and I went to summer school every summer trying to bring up my grades. As much as I wanted to be above average, I just couldn't seem to make it happen. I could see by the amount of time other kids put into studying that I had to work twice as hard as the next person. Most of my friends would read a page once and be able to comprehend what they read. I sometimes would have to read the same page three or four times to comprehend what I had just read.

I did, though, make the honor roll a couple of times, which brought me great satisfaction. There was nothing better than when the report cards came out and I was able to say to my friends that I had gotten a B average for that reporting period. It gave me self-confidence and the feeling that I, too, could do the same work as the rest of the students.

It was through hard work and tutors that I was able to make the academic honor roll. I can only tell you the feeling is like crossing the finish line first! Every time I tried and failed, I would think my teachers in grammar school were right, and I would never amount to anything. I was determined to show them they were wrong about me. I was learning probably subconsciously that if I wanted something badly enough and was willing to work hard, I could accomplish the task before me. With each accomplishment I was starting to gain some confidence!

Junior high was the first introduction to organized sports for me. There was baseball, football, and basketball. Soccer was just being introduced in the United States in 1959 -60. Most of the guys in my class were coordinated and had experience or had been to professional ball games with their dads. Many interacted with their fathers or older brothers and played catch. My dad worked six days a week to 5 p.m. He never had the time to throw a ball around with me. I can't ever remember him sitting at home on a Saturday or Sunday to watch a ball game of any kind on television. Once a year, though, he would take me and my friends for my birthday to a University of California college football game. So, my knowledge of sports was very limited.

What I learned about sports in my early years was from the guys and their fathers in the neighborhood. When it came to choosing teams, I was usually the last person chosen. Naturally, I never was made the captain of a team. The best athletes were always made captain and got to choose the players on their team. I was the kid that went long or played right field.

I really liked sports; I just didn't have the opportunity to hone the skills to be good. Like academics, I needed a base to work from. Occasionally, one of the dads in the neighborhood would let me play catch with him when he was throwing the ball to his son. But again, the stigma of my being uncoordinated and clumsy didn't inspire the others to want me on their team. Rejection in sports and academics doesn't make one very self-confident. Looking back, I must have been either tenacious or thick-skinned since I never gave up or quit. As junior high came to an end and high school began, I could only wonder what new adventures I would experience.

In 1961 a new high school opened in the Oakland hills. It was built on Skyline Boulevard, so naturally it was named Skyline High School. Along with its opening and its demographics it created a lot of political controversy and adversity in the city of Oakland. Up until 1961 all high school districts were made up of vertical boundaries starting from the top of the Oakland Hills and traversing in a vertical path to the Oakland estuary. Which area you lived in determined which high school you would attend.

Skyline High was a beautiful high school, state of the art. Instead of the vertical boundaries, a decision was made to create horizontal boundaries. A horizontal line was drawn across the hill area which represented the more affluent part of Oakland. Immediately, the politicians and newspapers were screaming "de facto-segregation". There were many demonstrations, and after I graduated, kids were bussed from the less influential areas to Skyline High. This was now, for me, the second new school I was to start in.

New schools have no traditions or history. Everyone was nervous and anxious because no one knew what to expect. There was no one to ask what high school was going to be like because no one had ever gone to this new school. It was like starting from the beginning. We students were told we would be the ones to create the traditions and customs that would be followed by students for years after we had graduated and moved on. My graduating class in 1964 had over seven hundred kids with a student body population of around 2,300 kids.

SKYLINE
HIGH SCHOOL
Class of 1964

Clyde
Batavia

CHAPTER VIII
A SPARK OF
SELF-CONFIDENCE

The summer before I started high school I was asked by the guys in our neighborhood if I was going to try out for the football team. I emphatically said, "no way". I didn't have much knowledge about the game and my history with sports was being uncoordinated. Over many days of being pestered by the guys, I finally said I would go with them to the try outs...new high school and all new sport teams. There must have been well over a hundred boys going out for the team. They had us run all kinds of drills and do lots of push-ups along with our running. For whatever reason, when the final cut was made, I was on the team. I was so surprised since most of my friends who were much more coordinated and good athletes did not make the team.

To this day I believe that was the moment I realized I could do anything I put my mind to. After all, for all these years I had been led to believe I was dumb and would never amount to anything. And yet, I was on the high school football team now. To top that off, it was a prestigious high school. The thought of being able to accomplish a goal made me realize that regardless of how difficult something might be, I could figure out a way to do it.

I believe that was a tremendous motivator for me. I was in no way a great athlete, and yet I held my own. I learned how to ski and belonged to the ski club. I threw the shot put in track. I was too small to be any good, but I competed on the second string. In my senior year when I could run for a student body office, I ran for treasurer of the high school and won.

It had become obvious to me that I could compete on the physical level, but academics were still a real challenge; and not being taught the basics in those early years was damaging to my ability to excel in academics. Junior year is when most of the guys turned sixteen and were able to get a driver's license. At fifteen and a half, you could get your learner's permit to drive. That required taking a written test. In those years, the high school also provided driver training, which you had to take before the physical driving test with the Department of Motor Vehicles test giver, who sat next to you in the car.

There was nothing I wanted more in the world than to get my learner's permit so I could drive. The thought of taking the written test scared me because I was afraid I wouldn't pass. I don't know if I had ever studied harder than I did for that written test. In California, now, they require people to take the written test once again when they reach age seventy. I studied for weeks. I did not want to fail. To this day I know I still have a difficult time taking tests. By the way, I got 100% on my written exam when I was fifteen-and-a-half and again at age seventy-two.

Skyline High School, due to its geographical location in Oakland, is where kids from the most affluent families attended. These children typically are high achievers. High achievers created a highly competitive environment. As is said, the cream rises to the top, and the top get into the best colleges of their choice. The mantra of the teachers at Skyline High was that if you didn't get accepted to the University of California, Stanford, Harvard, Yale or Princeton you didn't amount to much of anything.

The teachers were not shy about promoting getting into one of these schools and every time one of them talked about it, I would think I wasn't good enough. My parents, uncle, and just about everyone in our family had gone to the University of California, or CAL, as it is known. As I mentioned before, my earlier birthdays were spent with my dad taking my friends and me to the Cal football games and having lunch at his old fraternity house.

I really wanted to attend Cal. In the 1960's to be accepted there you had to complete what was called the A to F requirements. This meant you had to have 3 years of foreign language, chemistry, physics, algebra, geometry and trigonometry.

On top of completing those requirements you had to have a minimum of a 3.0 grade point average or a B. In the sixties there was only a four-point system of grading.

I went to summer school every year of high school and had tutors; yet no matter how hard I worked at it, I came up short at graduation. My grade point average was 2.8…no University of California for me. I felt like a flunky and was completely dejected. Once again, I couldn't make the grade. The teachers had done a good psychological brain washing on us students to make us think if we didn't go to a major university, we had failed. But I had also developed a sense that regardless of my academic deficiencies I could achieve anything I put my mind to. I thought if I went to junior college, I could then transfer to Cal.

I told my parents of my plan, thinking it was a pretty good one; but they had another one to lay on me. I guess they had been looking forward to my finally getting out of the house and going to college. Junior college was, therefore, not an option with my dad as I would still be living at home. He felt it was important for me to go away to college. He kept saying it would be the best time of my life.

One night he said, "Clyde, I want you to start applying to colleges." After I had lost the battle of words, he and I, but mainly he, filled out applications to several good colleges:

University of Oregon, Colorado, Washington, and Nevada. I applied to Nevada, as it appeared to be easier to get accepted. I thought if I didn't get into the other colleges at least I could tell my friends that I got accepted to the University of Nevada in Reno. When the letters arrived in the mail from the different universities, to my disbelief I had been accepted at all four schools. Once again, the scars that I carried with me from my grammar school days had contributed to my feeling that I wouldn't get into any colleges. Yet here I was having to decide where to go.

Don was going to Cal; Gary was off to Cal State, Hayward; Eddie, San Jose State; Tommy, junior college. Patty became a flight attendant for United Airlines. My decision was simple as Oregon, Washington, and Colorado, were too far away from my friends, so naturally I picked University of Nevada in Reno. I was near skiing at Squaw Valley and had a 3 hour drive to visit my friends in the Bay area. My thought process for choosing a university was probably not the best. Then again, I never thought for a second I would get accepted anywhere.

In the fall of September,1964, my parents drove me to Reno to the University of Nevada. I was dropped off at the dormitory and we said our good-byes. I was seventeen years old and on my own. Dorm life was an exciting new experience. Meals were served at what was called the dining hall. Breakfast, lunch, and dinner were available every day, except Sunday there was no dinner served. The dorm I was in was the newest at the university. There were four bedrooms in each unit with two guys in each room, two community bathrooms and a sitting area.

The first guys I met at the university were from Elko, Nevada. Compared to kids from the big city these guys were more like cowboys who liked to have fun. Some of these new acquaintances had high school graduating classes of 7 to 10 people, compared to my class of seven hundred plus students. Some had never seen the Pacific Ocean. You might say these were good old boys and they could be wild! But if they were your friends you could always count on them for help.

I wasn't at the school for more than four hours when these new friends said, "Come on with us. We're heading out to the local cat house," or as some would call it "a house of ill-repute".

CHAPTER IX
COLLEGE TIME

I n the State of Nevada certain counties have legalized prostitution. Just because I had been able to get rid of my label from grammar school of being a cut up, I still possessed that demon inside of me of loving to push the envelope and getting into mischief.

Getting into mischief seemed to follow me throughout my life. I can only guess it gave me a thrill to see how far I could push the envelope till it backfired on me. When I was little, if my mother said not to touch something because it was hot, I would immediately touch it and burn myself. That was my introduction to college life.

Because the university was small, everyone was included at many of the functions; and being Reno, the places that held these events never requested an ID. Therefore, you can imagine all these young seventeen and eighteen-year-old's purchasing alcohol. Dad was right. College life was great!

In the sixties at UNR (University of Nevada), freshmen were assigned a counselor. The counselor helped us choose classes we needed to fulfill our requirements for graduation. There were only two mandatory classes I had to take: English 1 and 2 and two years of R.O.T.C. (Reserve Officers Training Corps). I met with my counselor, told her I wanted to be a doctor, and she gave me an outline of what classes I needed to take.

At most universities, students had to pass the Subject A exam, before taking English 1and 2. The Subject A was to test your knowledge of writing and sentence construction and to determine if you could write properly. If you didn't pass, then you had to take remedial English better known as "bonehead English". Male students seemed to have more difficulty passing the Subject A, whereas more female students were better in passing it. The university gave you two chances to pass the test or you had to sit out the next semester.

I had missed out in my early years when I should have learned how to construct a proper sentence and use proper grammar. I just couldn't understand and grasp dangling participles, uses of apostrophes, run-on sentences, and all that goes with grammar. Because I didn't understand these concepts, I always wrote like I spoke, and still do. It has always caused me problems with my writing coherent sentences. I wondered what difference learning how to write correctly would make in my life. After all, what would I need this knowledge for out in the workplace? Years later my dad told me that he used to explain the importance of being able to write correctly to me and I would shrug my shoulders. He would question me by asking how I would get by if I couldn't write properly? Without missing a beat, I replied, "I will have a secretary." That is exactly how I managed. I have always had a secretary.

I did need to pass the Subject A to stay in college, and once again I found myself drowning in the academic arena. My parents paid for a tutor, and in the second semester I finally passed the test and went on to English 1 and 2. That was too close for comfort. Sitting out a semester would have been devastating to me.

During that second semester when I was enrolled in "bone head" English, it was evident to the professor I was having a difficult time understanding the subject matter. I received a message that my counselor wanted to see me. When we met, she informed me that I had been referred to her by my remedial English professor. My counselor said the university wanted me to be tested. I agreed and the testing was set up. When I was called back to her office to go over the results, I was politely told they showed that I only had a twenty percent chance of graduating. My counselor and university psychologist tried to convince me that college wasn't for everyone and I should seriously consider withdrawing. They also suggested that perhaps I should look into learning a trade. The test showed that I also had learning disabilities, including dyslexia.

This was the first time in my life I had learned I actually had a learning disability. It was determined when it came to multiple choice questions, even though I knew the material, instead of answering the question directly asked, I would read more into it than was necessary. Inevitably I would choose the wrong answer, proving that even though I knew the subject well I still might not pass a multiple-choice exam. I learned later that some people just don't test well on written exams.

In the sixties the university didn't have tutors for students with learning disabilities, as are offered today at most universities. Education in those days was pretty much one size fits all. If you didn't fit the mold then you floundered on your own. Once again I heard the same old theme I had been hearing since I could remember: "You won't make it or amount to anything."

I was crushed! The thought of failing and leaving the university hurt me to my core. I had worked so hard to get here and now I was being told I didn't belong. Most of my friends from my neighborhood were in college now. How could I ever go home and face them over summer vacation? I couldn't imagine the disappointment my parents would feel.

As my first semester came to end at UNR it was very common to sell books back to the ASUN (Associated Students University of Nevada) bookstore. The better condition of your book, the more money you would receive for it. I think the maximum you would get back was sixty percent, if the book was going to be used for the same class the next semester. On the way into the dining commons were rows of wire bookshelves to leave books on. I left my political science book on the shelves on my way into the dining hall, as I had planned to sell my books after lunch.

When I came out, my book was gone and a worn out political science book like mine was sitting in its place. I just figured that someone who had the same class swapped books, as my book was in mint condition, and they would get more money for it. It never entered my mind that someone who hadn't taken the class might have taken my book.

I went to the bookstore to sell what I thought was now my book. A few days later I was called to the dean of men's office. Dean Hawthorne asked me if I had sold a book he had which looked like the one I'd sold. I told him I had sold it. He said it was a very serious violation of the University code. I explained how I had come into possession of the book, which didn't seem to make any difference to him. He said he would have to suspend me from the University for a semester for my action or that I could go before the student judicial council to see what they would say.

Needless to say, I was very upset, and my folks were equally upset. I had not intentionally meant to do anything wrong, but here I was again back in grammar school hearing those same words that I would never amount to anything. Instead of the red chair in the corner I was going to be kicked out for a semester.

I felt sick to my stomach. I chose to go before the student judicial council, who sentenced me to "disciplinary probation" for the rest of my time at the university. I was relieved with the outcome as it allowed me to stay in school. I knew I now had the responsibility of staying out of any trouble the rest of my time at UNR. I believe that had the decision by the judicial court been suspension, it would have changed my life's path and my accomplishments to come.

No semester credits toward graduating were given to me for the year I spent trying to pass the Subject A exam, but they went down on my transcript as semester hours. To graduate you needed a certain number of credits for specific classes. Therefore, I had already fallen behind six credits at the end of my first year of college.

CHAPTER X
SELECTIVE SERVICE BOARD

The University of Nevada was a land grant school, and therefore all male students were required to take ROTC (Reserve Officers Training Corps) for their first two years. This was a one credit course. Twice a week, men had to dress in army dress green uniforms and drill. I hated this as much as I had disliked grammar school. I barely passed with a D-. I had a problem with following what I thought were ridiculous orders.

My other classes the first couple of years were geared toward getting into medical school. I had to take foreign language, biology, and lots of chemistry. The chemistry called for labs in the afternoons. I liked chemistry, but when ski season came along in the winter, I found the chemistry labs were interfering with my skiing. By 1966 I realized my grades would never get me accepted to a medical school. The easiest thing for me would be to switch my major to business. After all, our family had a scrap business and sold new and used industrial machinery. I had worked for my father during my summers and had enjoyed it. If I couldn't be a doctor, I figured I could fall back on the family business.

Meanwhile, I was plugging along and maintaining grades to keep me in school. There was no doubt that business school was much easier with no labs to contend with.

The escalation of the Vietnam War began during my fall semester of 1967. Every evening the news was bringing the war up close and personal. The United States had instituted the Selective Service Act in 1940, and the last draft selection ended on December 7, 1972. This meant that all men must register for the military draft on their eighteenth birthday. Overnight, men in that age group were being called up to take their physical to be drafted into the Army. This included some of my friends who were already 18 being called to the Oakland Army Base for their induction.

It seemed like everyone was looking for ways to avoid being sent to fight a war in a place called Vietnam. Overnight the National Guard, Army Reserves, and Air National Guard were filling to capacity. Everyone was scrambling for a way to stay out of the draft or at least finish college first. All over America people were watching this war escalate and seeing the casualties mounting daily from our tv sets, where casualties were reported every night. Everyone knew someone who was being sent to Vietnam. It was a frightening time, especially for mothers and fathers of sons who were recruited.

The Selective Service Board offered deferments if certain requirements were met. If you were in college, married, or had a health issue you would be given a different classification. I, like many of my friends, thought we were safe since we were in college. We thought we would qualify for a 2S deferment which was a deferment

46

for students. This is where it gets a bit tricky. Every state had its own requirements for qualifying for a deferment.

The State of California required that to receive a college deferment one must maintain a minimum of fifteen semester credits. Other states only required fifteen semester hours. Earlier I mentioned I took "bone head" English for two semesters. Bone head English only counted as semester hours not semester credits. Most of my friends and I didn't understand the difference between semester hours and credits. Neither did most of us male students in California.

Therefore, at the end of my first year I lacked six semester credits for a 2S student deferment. Once again, I felt the same fear I had when I was sent to the cloak room to sit in the corner in the little red chair. Now it might cost me my life!

Unfortunately, for me, my family had no political pull, and my options were quickly closing. Some of my friends' parents got doctors to falsify records making them not fit to serve, and some ran to Canada to avoid induction. The country was in chaos as the nightly news was showing the war and death count climbing higher day by day. This was the first time in history people were seeing war up close in the privacy of their living rooms. The reality of what war does and looks like was not something civilians liked seeing.

CHAPTER XI
SAVED BY ROTC

My one option as I saw it was to try and get into the upper division ROTC program, which was called advanced ROTC. UNR only had 35 slots for upper division. The University of California, I believe, had 75 slots. The slots for upper division had to do with the size of the universities. At UNR the slots were being filled fast, first to the school athletes. I, having disliked and done very poorly in ROTC, now found myself at Hartman Hall, the ROTC building on campus. I went in to see Major Halverson to find out what I needed to do to get accepted to the upper division program. He told me my grades were sub-standard. I had one semester of ROTC left. The major said there was a volunteer program called the "Counter Guerrilla Program" that was available to the lower classmen. He told me joining the program would certainly look good on my record, and if I brought up my grade for the last semester, I might have a chance to get an advanced ROTC slot. He didn't want to raise my hopes, since my grades were so bad.

The guys who were involved in this program were the guys who thought they were warriors and couldn't wait to go over and fight in a war. These were the gung-ho guys! I just wanted to graduate and stay alive. I was a lover not fighter! Major Halverson said I had one semester left and if I could show that I had the making of an officer, there might be a slot for me.

I joined the counter guerrilla group. We played war games on the weekends, and Easter vacation was spent at a military base. At the end of the semester I was called in to Major Halverson's office. He told me I had shown exemplary leadership and command in the field, and that I would be given a slot as long as I kept up the good work and kept showing them I was deserving of a commission. In fact, I was made company commander of the first new group to start the first year of the advanced cadet class. I was impressed with my accomplishment. After all, I never got to be a team captain, and now I was.

Before being given the oath to the United States and admitted to the advanced program, the Army did a NAC (National Agency Check) on you. This was a background check on you, your parents, and grandparents. The military wanted to be sure there were no subversive organizations you or your family might be associated with. What did come up was my disciplinary probation due to the book incident I mentioned previously. The fact that I was on disciplinary probation would be cause enough not to allow me into the upper division ROTC program. I was told that I would have to appeal my probation. I did appeal to the university's judicial council. I am not sure what happened, but the ROTC department was able to get the remainder of my probation waived. At least I was now guaranteed to graduate from college.

All of us in advanced ROTC were issued an 1D deferment meaning the military was deferring our service commitment. The next two years of ROTC we received a government check of fifty dollars on the first of every month. You can bet that fifty-dollar check went directly for beer!

The curriculum was different for upper ROTC. Military history, map reading, time on the firing range, and weekends at rifle range, were all used to train us in the latest tactics being used in Vietnam. Spring break was spent at Fort Ord, an Army base for training. I excelled in field training, which I found interesting and liked. The whole time we were training we were convinced that this war would be over before we graduated. Then February of 1968, the Tet offensive happened in Vietnam.

It was like someone dumped gasoline on the fire. The military was escalating at full speed. Everyone was looking for a way to delay their graduation which meant delaying being commissioned in the military. I changed my major from business to hospital administration. This would buy me another year at UNR. In late 1967, the Army awarded branch assignments to those who still had a year before graduation. I received what I had applied for: the medical service branch. The Pentagon sent me a little box with Second Lieutenant bars and my branch insignia, which I wore on my uniform. Because my branch was to be Medical Service Corps, the Army would

UNIVERSITY OF NEVADA
RENO — LAS VEGAS

PAGE 1 OF 2 PA

COLLEGE					
A/A/A Bus.Adm.6/66					
MAJOR Management					
MINOR					
DEGREE B.S. in Bus.Ad.					
DATE GRANTED 6/7/69					
CREDITS REQUIRED 128			G.P.A.	2.08	
DESCRIPTION	CODE	DEPT.	NUMBER	CREDIT	GRA
PLANE TRIGONOMETRY		MATH	102	2	
2ND YR BASIC BR GEN		MIL	202	1	
PE ACT BOWLING		P ED	100	1	
SEM 12 12 19 1.58		CUM	51 51	98	

send me after my graduation to Baylor University for a master's degree in hospital administration.

I thought I had outsmarted the Army. I changed my major so that I now would graduate in the spring of 1969, a year later than I was supposed to. I had bought myself another year and had been awarded the branch I desired. I was feeling pretty good about this. How naive of me! Due to the Tet offensive of 68' the Pentagon sent out

Orders to Ft. Benning and active duty.

orders to all of us who had delayed graduation and commissioning one year. We would have to re-apply for our branch assignments. Everyone re-applied for the branch they had previously received. When the branch assignments came back from the Pentagon everyone got the army's choice of infantry.

My dad had tried to convince me from the day I got into the advanced ROTC program to try and get into the NROTC (Naval Reserve Officer Training Corps). I kept telling my dad that this was the new army, not to worry, I would be in the medical corps. Seems the older I got the smarter my dad got! Panic became the order of the day. We all thought we had been given a death sentence and that we would die in some humid hot jungle ten thousand miles from home!

Perhaps that was the motivation for us cadets to hit the nearest bar and consume way too much booze. The more we drank the braver we all got. It wasn't long before all 7 of us went up to Hartman Hall. We marched into Major Halverson's office and requested to serve as Airborne Rangers. He tried to talk us out of it, but the alcohol took over any reasoning we might have had that day. Seven of us had requested two different schools. When the paperwork came back from the army, I was the only one who was selected for Airborne Ranger school. Before diplomas were handed out at graduation, all those having completed advanced ROTC were asked to stand and take the oath of the United States' military. At the end of the oath we were all commissioned Second Lieutenants in the U.S. Army. That is the way it was done in 1969.

CHAPTER XII

OFF TO FORT BENNING GEORGIA

I was barely keeping my head above water as far as academics went. I was narrowly maintaining a C average. I could not afford to get one bad grade, or I would fall below a 2.0 average and would not be able to graduate on time. That would have meant delaying graduating and my getting my commission. I certainly didn't want to take summer school to make up a grade. Once again, the bad feeling of being held behind and not graduating with my class was very distasteful. I managed to graduate with a 2.08 grade point average. In my mind, it was like they say: "A win is a win". The 2.08 GPA got me across the academic finish line. I enjoyed the thought of never again having to open a book or be in a classroom environment. How very wrong I was.

Upon graduation I received my orders to report to Fort Benning, Georgia. My orders read that I must report before but not later than August 17, 1969, for IOBC (Infantry Officer Basic Course). In 1967 my parents had bought me a used 1964 Oldsmobile Cutlass to go back and forth to college. I loved the car and still had it through my time in the military. I planned to drive it back to Fort Benning.

In those days air conditioning was an option, not a standard feature in cars. That time of year I would be driving from Oakland, California, to Georgia when it was very hot, and my car had no air conditioning. One of our neighbors owned an auto parts store. I asked him about how difficult it would be to install an after-market air conditioning unit in my car. He said if I could read, I should be able to do it myself, but he offered to assist me on the more complicated parts of the installation. I think the unit cost around three hundred dollars. This might have been the first time that I saw the practical use of reading.

Due to my difficulties with comprehension, I had to read the installation manual several times. I almost completed the entire installation on my own. Our neighbor was very helpful with the wiring portion. I can remember standing back when I started up my Cutlass and turning on the switch and feeling the cool air coming out of the unit, which I had installed under the dashboard. Wow! It worked, and now I would be cool on my long drive. I can remember thinking how useful being able to read could be. I was full of pride, as it was another accomplishment under my belt. I couldn't wait to show all my friends what I had been able to do.

I said good-bye to my parents and my fiancée the night before I left. Before the sun rose on August 8, 1969, I headed toward Georgia. There were no cell phones or GPS systems yet. Therefore, I had joined AAA (American Automobile Association). I had gone to their office where they outlined with a felt pen on paper maps the best route to my destination.

It is almost 2,500 miles from Oakland, California, to Fort Benning, Georgia. I had no idea what to expect. This was going to be a new adventure and I was all by myself. I remember my stomach being a little queasy as I rolled onto to the highway. Two days later I was pulling up to the front gate at Fort Benning. An enlisted man approached my car and asked for my orders. He took them into the booth at the gate. When he returned, he saluted me, my first real salute as an army officer. He called me "Sir", and he gave me directions to the location of the company I had been assigned. I found the orderly office and was assigned a room and roommate. His name was Don, and he was from Columbus, Ohio.

For the next three months, we would be roommates. Officers that were not married usually lived on base. Officer quarters were in large concrete buildings called halls. Each company was assigned to a different hall. Each room housed two men each with private bathroom. The halls looked like large three-story motels. On the bottom floor when you entered your hall was the orderly room that was staffed twenty-four hours a day, seven days a week. Each officer's name would be on the duty list. When your name came up, it was your turn to be on duty all night.

One night while I was staff duty officer, I was having a hard time staying awake. I started snooping at all the different forms and came across one that read "Voluntary Indefinite". The war was now raging in Vietnam and the army needed to retain officers, especially infantry officers. To entice them to stay in longer than their two-year obligation, the army came up with a plan called "Voluntary Indefinite". If you signed to go "vol and def" the army would guarantee you two years of your choice as long as there was a slot available. It also meant you would be released from active duty when the army saw fit. I was still betting this war would shortly come to end and I would be released from active duty, since the army no longer needed me.

I called the Pentagon to talk to Major Wickman, the adviser in charge of all of us Infantry Lieutenants. He asked where I wanted to go for my first duty assignment. Having gone to UNR and having been a skier and a ski instructor, I had heard that a couple of UNR lieutenants who graduated before me were teaching skiing in Alaska, Fort Carson, Colorado, and Augsburg, Germany. I saw that Fort Greely, Alaska, had the NWTC (Northern Warfare Training Command). That was perfect, I thought, plus it was an accompanied tour. That meant you could bring your wife. Remember there were no computers in those days, and I figured they would either forget where I was or not send someone stationed in Alaska to Vietnam. Major Wickman called me some days later and said he had a slot and was sending the papers for me to sign. Alaska was a great tour, which would allow my wife and me time to build our relationship as husband and wife. Two years later to the date, I received my orders for Vietnam.

The orderly room was where the company commander's office was and where all records, forms and daily training assignments were posted. It was each officer's responsibility to read the training schedule and be prepared for the next day. The training schedule informed us what dress would be required and everything we needed to know. The quarters were comfortable enough, though we did not always get to sleep in them if we were on maneuvers. Each hall had its own officers' mess hall, which is where we went for meals.

My thinking was that once I was in the army, all the training would be outside in the field. After all, the infantry fights outdoors. I could not have been more incorrect. Sixty percent of our training would be conducted outside and forty percent in the class- room. Here I was again back in a school environment. Even though we were commissioned as officers we would all have to pass the IOBC exam (Infantry Officers Basic Course), which was composed of written as well as field tests. Oh boy, I was not looking forward to all the reading. Fortunately, there were no papers to be turned in, so I didn't have to worry about writing any. That still left having to take a written test which was always difficult for me and which gave me a reason to be concerned. There is no agency or company that has more manuals than the U.S. Army. The army has a manual for everything you can possibly think of, from digging a fox hole to sanitation in the field.

For just about every subject that came up, we were handed a manual to read and to be tested on. I thought I was done with the classroom situation, and here I was struggling to stay on top of the reading as well as the physical training. My lack of grammar school education was rearing its ugly head again. Every time I thought I was moving forward with my life the reality was that I just couldn't escape the basics of grammar school. Naturally, when we took tests, the questions always seemed to be more about seeing if we had read the material than what the important part was to know.

About halfway through IOBC, the company commander called me to his office and told me that he was worried about my written scores. They were below what was needed to pass the IOBC. On the other hand, he told me my field training and leadership skills were excellent, and I was at the top of our company. He told me to get those test scores up. That same old song was repeating itself once again. I hated reading and to this day

I seldom read for pleasure. When you don't have a good base to build on, it is pure misery.

I had received orders to go to Airborne school after graduating from IOBC. Airborne school would buy me another month at Fort Benning. I was engaged to be married February 22, 1970. We got married and we are still married today. Meanwhile, I was still doing everything in my power to delay being sent off to Vietnam right away as a Second Lieutenant. Therefore, it was paramount for me to graduate from IOBC.

Test scores at IOBC were graded on a curve, but I was still on the wrong side of it. I tried to convince the company commander to give me the test orally. I was sure I would pass with flying colors if I could do it that way. Unfortunately, I learned very quickly there is a right way, a wrong way, and the army way. The major in charge said I was to sit between Jim and Mike, who just happened to have become my friends. These two guys also just happened to be West Point graduates. They knew the book material inside and out. The test as I remember was mostly multiple choice. I was told if I wasn't certain of the correct answers, I was to look over at their test papers. Jim and Mike told me later they were okay with me using their answers to check mine. Needless to say, and lucky for me, I passed, and headed on to Airborne school.

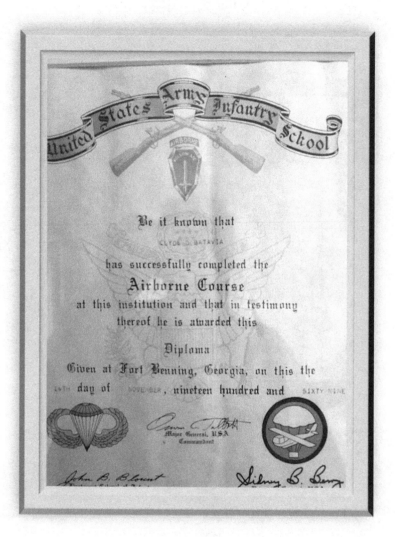

CHAPTER XIII
FORT GREELY ALASKA

I found Airborne school exciting. The thought of jumping out of an airplane gave me a rush. The best part was that there were no books, no written tests, just pure physical ability and pure toughness like I had never experienced. I had thought football practice was hard. Airborne school was on another level. At the time I did not realize it, but this was a real confidence building experience. We started out with a class of over eight hundred enlisted men and officers. Airborne school was run at Fort Benning and was a joint military school, as it trained the Army, Marines, Navy Seals, and Air Force.

The first two weeks were grueling. The sergeants pretty much ran Airborne school, and they took great enjoyment having the opportunity to harass the officers for three weeks with no repercussions to them personally. The third week was called jump week, and we jumped every day out of different types of aircraft. On graduation day there were barely four hundred of us left. They pinned our Jump Wings on us. I think all four hundred of us thought there was nothing we couldn't do!

After completing the toughest, most physically demanding thing I had ever done, it left me with the confidence of knowing I could conquer anything that came my way. When you came across another serviceman, no matter where or what uniform of their branch, if they wore the Jump Wings, you would say as you passed them, "AIRBORNE!", and they would respond, "ALL THE WAY".

Even today when I travel and I see a person wearing the uniform with Jump Wings, I will say "Airborne" and will always get the reply of "All the way"! It is a definite bond among us servicemen and women.

I packed up the car, bought thirty hamburgers and lots of french fries and headed to Oakland, California, to see my parents and fiancée before heading to Alaska. I drove all day and night non-stop. After all, having completed Airborne school, what was a drive of 2,500 miles but a piece of cake! I only had a few days to get to Fort Greely, and I still needed to ship my car from Seattle to Anchorage.

After a few days at home, I headed for Seattle. Sending an automobile by ship to a destination has many requirements. I had to find the correct port per the army instructions. At the port I was given a booklet that entailed having to read instructions and follow them. I also needed to rent a motel room for a night so I could get everything organized. I read the instructions and was able to get my car prepared properly for shipping. Then after dropping it off, I had to arrange to get myself to the Seattle airport and fly in uniform per my orders. What I didn't realize was that each time I was accomplishing these real-life tasks, I was growing in confidence and experiences. My reading comprehension was notably getting better, as everything required my being able to read and comprehend what I had read. I learned there was no embarrassment in asking someone for help if I was having trouble comprehending the instructions.

I arrived at the Fairbanks, Alaska airport in November 1969, at 9 p.m. I was in my dress greens. The airport consisted of a Quonset hut, as a new airport terminal was in the process of being built. The airport personnel wheeled out mobile stairs so the passengers could disembark from the plane. It was about forty below zero or maybe 50. I had not been issued my army winter clothing yet. As I climbed down the stairs, the first thing I noticed was my nostrils sticking together. When the outside temperature is that cold and you breathe in through your nose, your nostrils stick together from the moist air inside of them. Winter clothing was heavy field pants, wool shirt and parka with fur hood, and field VB boots. The VB stood for vapor barrier. These boots had a valve to adjust air between layers.

The army, in those days, customarily assigned arriving officers a sponsor. Your sponsor was to help you get acquainted with the military post and help you settle into your new surroundings. There, waiting for me in the Quonset hut, were Mike and his wife Sue. They had driven up from Fort Greely some one hundred miles south of Fairbanks. I received a very warm welcome from them. They told me that we would spend the night in Fairbanks at another friend's quarters at Fort Wainwright.

I quickly learned that traveling at night in the winter was not advisable in Alaska. If your car broke down, you could freeze to death in short order. Mike and Sue informed me that in the winter it was Alaska state law that drivers had to have a sleeping bag for each occupant in the car and food to survive. In the winter if we were driving and came upon a car broken down, it was the law that we must stop and render assistance. It would get so cold where we were stationed, Mike told me when we got in our car, we were to make sure we had two sets of keys.

You never turned your car off because it would freeze. Therefore, you would leave the car running and locked, and you would have the second set to reopen the door.

We left early the next morning from Fort Wainwright and headed south to Fort Greely. I signed in at the headquarters' office and was quickly introduced to several officers. I was told to get settled in and go down to Supply and draw a winter uniform from the quarter master. I was instructed to report in the morning to meet the post commander, who was a full bird colonel, the rank below general.

The next morning, I reported for duty and was led in to meet the post commander. I was asked to have a seat and we exchanged some pleasantries. He asked me questions about myself. He said he had heard that I taught skiing.

Fort Greely was comprised of a garrison and three other attachments, NWTC (Northern Warfare Training Center), ATC (Arctic Testing Center), and a unit that ran the nuclear power plant on post. I was told that the commander of the NWTC wanted me assigned to him because of I was a skier. My sponsor on the way to Fort Greely had told me teaching skiing in the army had no similarity at all to that of the alpine skiing I knew from skiing at Squaw Valley.

Mike said I would be living out in the woods like a bear. When the post commander offered me the choice of being assigned to NTWC or taking the IO job (Information Officer), though I had no idea of what was required as the Information Officer, I knew I was going back to Oakland to get married in a couple of months. I didn't want to be living out in the woods having just married, so with a straight face I said to the commander, "I've been skiing all my life. I thought I would learn something different being in the army". He told me it was a position that required a major in rank, but due to the shortage of officers because of the war raging in Vietnam, I would be the new IO as a Second Lieutenant.

The IO at Fort Greely had responsibilities which I had no experience in nor had I been to the Army School for Information Officers at Fort Benjamin Harrison in Indiana. I was given a quick overview of what the duties were and what was expected of the IO. After a quick discussion I was sent on my way to my first job in the U.S. Army.

When I walked into my office, I was met by my Sergeant, who introduced me to the rest of the men that would report to me. Sergeant Arron went over each of the men's jobs and their area of responsibility. As Sergeant Arron escorted me through the building to show me around, I saw a large area that looked like a television studio, which it was.

To my surprise I learned because of Fort Greely being in a very remote area with no radio or television nearby and the nearest city some hundreds of miles away. Delta Junction was the closest thing we had to resemble a city. Delta Junction was where the Alcan Highway and Richardson Highway intersected. The Alcan Highway and Richardson Highway were the two major highways in Alaska in 1969.

CHAPTER XIV

BEING THE
INFORMATION OFFICER

The military had something called Armed Forces Radio Services (AFRS). This went back to World War II. When AFRS first came out there was no television. Later on, it was called Armed Forces Radio & Television Services (AFRS&TV). Today it is called AFN (Armed Forces Network). The military had a contract with Hollywood to furnish television shows and movies. Every quarter I would send one of the television crew to Hollywood to pick out movies and TV shows. Naturally, the choices Hollywood provided were the old, old shows and movies.

Delta Junction was about five miles from Fort Greely and because it didn't have radio or television and was close to the military installation in 1969, there was a law that the military installation must boost its signal so the nearest civilian area could receive that signal. We were to make sure our signal strength was strong enough for Delta Junction to receive radio and television!

What did I know about running a live television and radio network? Absolutely nothing! The moment I was assigned to my bachelor quarters, the engineers were there wiring it with a video monitor and speakers so I would be able to monitor the facility at all times. The television came on at noon every day and signed off at midnight. It was a one station operation. At midnight, when the station went off the air, it showed a picture of the American flag waving while the national anthem was played. If for any reason that television went down for any period of time, my phone would soon be ringing off the hook with the mothers on base wanting to know what had happened.

I also was in charge, as the IO, of writing all press releases and accompanying the post commander to all joint military briefings and meetings. I had the responsibility of making sure whatever information the post commander wanted disbursed got out to everyone on the military post. Fort Greely, like most military installations, had a post newspaper which came under my control.

When I learned some of the responsibilities that came along with being the Information Officer, panic set in. I started to wonder how in the world I would be able to do this job. Reading and writing were my worst subjects all through my education and had been difficult for me. I was thinking that living out in the arctic teaching skiing might have been a better choice. Now everything having to do with my first job assignment was dependent on my reading and writing skills.

Remember, I mentioned earlier in the book that the army has manuals for everything? I asked my Sergeant to get me the manuals for running a television station, radio station and newspaper. I must admit the army's manuals described how and what not to do. When my Sergeant returned some hours later, he had a stack of manuals, including how to write military press releases. Fortunately for me, there were few distractions, so I hunkered down in my office.

It was dark day and night and below zero most days. I wasn't getting married until February twenty-second so I decided, in the meantime, I would do the best I could. I had learned by now that there were ways to get answers other than the normal way of reading and being able to comprehend what was written.

The first thing I did was interview the men who were working for me. I had each of them teach me their job. I figured if I had hands-on working knowledge, then at least I could speak intelligently about each operation regarding the newspaper, radio, and television. Meanwhile, I started reading the manuals which really helped me comprehend after having the men explain what their jobs were and the responsibilities associated with them. Since I have learning difficulties, especially in reading and comprehension areas, I would find myself reading the same page over and over; and if I still didn't understand the subject, I would write it down and ask one of my men who would have the answer.

I spent every waking moment reading page by page of each manual very slowly until I finally got through all of them. Fortunately, when I had to cut press releases, I could have one of my men correct my spelling. Sometimes they would suggest a better way to write the release. The men that were assigned to the information office were all college graduates and were intelligent people. After a few weeks I had the office running very efficiently. I succeeded even with all the reading of the manuals. What I had learned, I was able to put into practical use. I think, looking back, I was more afraid of failing at my first job and not wanting to be labeled, as in my early years, a "screw up". It motivated me into applying myself one hundred and ten percent.

Whether I realized it or not, by having to read and comprehend what I read and then put it into use, I was increasing my reading and comprehension skills. I am not sure I realized it then, but my reading speed was also being enhanced. As I think back now, it was like an athlete who, the more he practices, the better he gets. By no means was this a fix, but it was giving me confidence that I could understand what I read, even though it was painful, time consuming, and difficult.

February rolled around and I took leave to head back to Oakland to get married. We went on our honeymoon, then we headed up to Fort Greely. While I was gone a school trained information officer had arrived and the post commander had been relieved. I was to be moved to Northern Warfare Training Center (NWTC). The deputy post commander called me into his office and said that Fort Greely was going to get a new post commander shortly. Lt. Col. Williamson told me since I had done such a good job at being the IO, the post commander had awarded me the MOS (Military Occupational Specialty) award. That MOS stays on your record forever. It shows up just as if you had gone to IO school at Fort Benjamin. I was now classified as an Infantry Officer and Information Officer which allowed me to work in either specialty.

Unfortunately, the colonel for NWTC was a full bird colonel and outranked the deputy post commander who was a lieutenant colonel. The colonel wanted me under his command because I had taught skiing. I was told not to worry, that I would not be assigned to NWTC once the new post commander arrived. After he arrived, I was

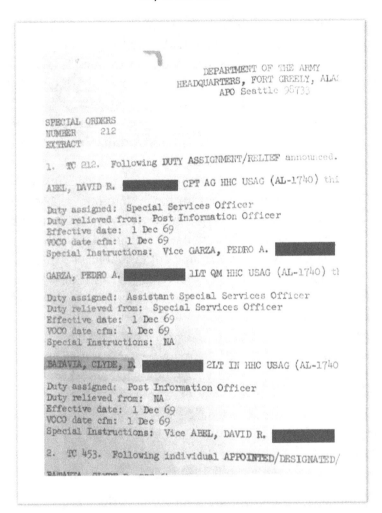

moved back to the garrison company, where I was told I would be taking over Special Services for Fort Greely.

I had no idea what running Special Services entailed. As it turned out it was like running a business. Everything and anything that had to do with morale of the troops came under the heading of Special Services. This included the post theater, automobile shop, wood shop, metal shop, service club, fishing camps, ski area, boys and girl scouts, teen club, rental of sports equipment, boats, snowmobiles, trailers, etc. I had a full-time comptroller, civilian and military personnel working for me. This was a natural fit for me, as my family had a business which I had worked in during my summer vacations.

The commanding general for the Alaskan command was Major General James F. Hollingsworth. His reputation was that he thought he was the General Patton of the Vietnam War. He was one tough son-of-a-bitch. He would relieve an officer on the spot for the least minor offense. He was known as the men's general! He was adamant that when an enlisted man had time off, he should have the best recreational activities and equipment available.

God help the Special Services Officer if an enlisted man took out a boat, camper, or snowmobile and it didn't function correctly. General Hollingsworth would show up unannounced and have the Special Services Officer accompany him to one of the many rental facilities on base. The general would point to an item. It could be a boat, motor, snow machine, camper, snowmobile, or anything else, and ask when maintenance was last done on that item. His inspections were always a surprise. You never knew at which post or base he would appear. The only warning you got was a call from another Special Services Officer from another post or base in Alaska letting you know the general had just left their facility and might be on his way. Usually, the officer making the call had just been relieved of duty.

CHAPTER XV
ORDERED TO VIETNAM

Once I knew what General Hollingsworth expected of his special services officers and what got some of them relieved, I went into hyper-speed. I came up with a card indexing system for all items. When I took over, there was little if any information regarding maintenance or service of rental items for the troops. My men worked day and night and, in a short amount of time, we had everything regarding maintenance on index cards along with a maintenance program. We set up an ordering program for auto parts, so when men came in to use the auto shop, we would have the common, necessary parts in stock.

One day the post commander called me to his office. When I walked in, General Hollingsworth was there. For a lieutenant to be in the presence of a general was a rare occurrence and, needless to say, an intimidating one. He ordered me to accompany him to the building where the boats, trailers, snowmobiles and outboard engines were stored. I walked into the building with him and he randomly pointed to one of the snowmobiles and asked me when it was last serviced. I turned to the man in charge and repeated the question. He opened the index file, pulled out the card and gave the general the information he had requested.

DEPARTMENT OF THE ARMY
Headquarters, 23d Infantry Division (Americal)
APO San Francisco 96374

SPECIAL ORDERS
NUMBER   285
EXTRACT

9 TC 420. By direction of the President, following individual PROMOTED/
ADVANCED and COMMISSIONED in the Army of the United States.

BATAVIA, CLYDE D. ███████ 1LT 1542 IBC 23d Inf Div (Americal) IN

Authority: 10 USC 3442 and 3447
Grade (from, to): 1LT to CPT
Appointed by: CG, 23d Inf Div
Effective date: 10 October 1971
Date of rank: 10 October 1971

FOR THE COMMANDER:

OFFICIAL: WILLIAM R. RICHARDSON
                                            Colonel, GS
                                            Chief of Staff

H. W. QUINN
CPT, AGC
Asst AG

DISTRIBUTION:
5-Indiv Conc
40-AVDP-AOPB
10-AVDP-AINO
5-AVDP-AOPB (MR)
5-AVDT-AJM
5-AVDP-PC
5-HHC 23d Inf Div

SPECIAL DISTRIBUTION:
1-Director, OPO, ATTN: OPD-IP, Washington, D.C. 20315
1-TAGO, ATTN: AGPT-P
1-TAGO, ATTN: AGPB-I
1-TAGO, ATTN: AGRE-PD

The general turned to me said, "Outstanding! It's about time we had someone who knows how to run Special Services".

From that day on, I was his man and it followed me during my time in the military. When the generals would be coming back to the states from Vietnam on their way to Washington D.C. or to a new command, due to the flight distance from Vietnam, they would stop in Alaska for refueling and an overnight stay. I would get a call from General Hollingsworth to set up a fishing trip for these generals or some dignitary. One of my sergeants would set it up, and I would make sure we had the libations they liked on the boat. The more I was with these high-ranking officers, the more comfortable I was becoming. Looking back, I realize these accomplishments were

DEPARTMENT OF THE ARMY
Headquarters, 196th Infantry Brigade
APO San Francisco 96256

24 Nov 69

SPECIAL ORDERS
NUMBER   328
EXTRACT

65 TC 200. Following reassignment directed. Individual will proc
PERMANENT CHANGE OF STATION as indicated.

BATAVIA, CLYDE L., 5██████████CPT 71542 HHC 196th Inf Bde (A.F3E.)

ADMINISTRATIVE ACCOUNTING DATA
Auth: VOCG (MAJ Kelly, HC USARV)
Aloc: NA
DPO Cal No: NA
Lv Adrs: NA
PCS ACC: 3F02

FOR THE INDIVIDUAL
Assigned to: H, USARV Special Troops APO 96291
EDCSA: 25 Nov 71
Reporting date: 25 Nov 71
Leave data: NA
Special Instructions: Individual will comply with the following let
of 196th Infantry Brigade Supplemental Instru
C, D, E, F, G, H, I.
(a) PDY with Special Service Agency (5000)

FOR THE COMMANDER

OFFICIAL

H.W. RICHMOND
1LT, AGC
Asst AG

WARNER J. GOODWIN
Colonel, Infantry
Deputy Brigade Commander

Orders to Vietnam

building confidence in me I didn't realize I had. Apparently, my confidence and my performance were being recognized and I was promoted to the rank of "captain" shortly after.

As my guaranteed two years were coming to a close and the war was still going on, I received my orders to go to Vietnam. In most cases, when officers got orders, they went to what was called a REPO Depot (Replacement Personnel Office) and from there were sent where an officer was needed. The year was 1971 and the war was very unpopular in the States. This was the beginning of getting our troops out of Vietnam and back to the United States. The military was starting to downsize, though the war wasn't over until 1975.

This was not the case for me because I had been awarded the Information Officer MOS at Fort Greely. The military needed 200 information officers in Vietnam, and I was on direct orders to be the Information Officer for the Twenty-third Infantry Division. The Twenty-third Infantry Division was located near Chu Lai. Chu Lai was where the My Lai incident occurred. I was learning in the army you don't put a lot of credence on what your orders might say. Orders change rapidly depending on the needs at the time.

Major General Crossen had just taken over the command of the 23rd. He decided I was going to the Tactical Operations Center (TOC) as the Administration Officer. The TOC was underground in a bunker setting. Every time you entered you had to show your ID to the Military Police (MP) on guard. This is where you receive fire mission plans and where briefings and statistics were constantly being done and redone.

CPT. CLYDE D. BATAVIA
CHU LAI, VIETNAM 1971

My job was to put what information was collected into a briefing form. I would brief the White House representatives daily as well as at any time visiting dignitaries requested it. I had two lieutenants and a couple of sergeants who gathered the information as it came in. My men would provide me with the steady stream of information they were receiving from the units in the field. I would put it into a written briefing and submit it to a major for approval. Once approved I would give the briefing to everyone who needed it. Once again, I found myself accomplishing skills that have always been difficult for me.

The 23rd Infantry Division was the largest division during the Vietnam War and was soon to stand down and its colors sent back to the United States. The who's who of the Vietnam war were present at the stand down ceremony of the 23rd Infantry Division. General Abrams, the Commanding General of Vietnam and all the high-ranking Vietnamese generals were also present.

While watching the pomp and circumstance taking place, I felt a hard slap on my back. I turned around with clenched fists and to my amazement there stood General Hollingsworth. He wanted to know what I was going to be assigned to next. I saluted him as did my buddies standing alongside me. I said they were sending me up to Da Nang for assignment.

I asked what he was doing, and he replied, "They're giving me my third star and I am taking over the third region of Vietnam". The general asked if I was still as good as I had been when I was a Special Services officer.

I said, "Absolutely Sir!"

He asked if I would like to take over sports for the entire third region of Vietnam. I would have signed up for another year for that job!

He turned to his aide, a full bird colonel, and said: "Write the captain an order to get his ass down to Plantation". The colonel pulled out a notebook and wrote the order right there on the spot. Then he said, "Get your ass down to Plantation," which was going to be his new headquarters (HQ).

The next day was my twenty-fifth birthday. I made my way to the airfield to wait for a flight that was heading to Tan Son Nhut Air Force Base. I spent the day and night on the concrete floor of the airfield. The next morning an Air Force sergeant came up to me and said he had a flight heading south to Tan Son Nhut. I jumped on the C-130 cargo plane and was off. In war time there were no seats in the planes, so you sat on the floor and held onto a cargo strap that went across the floor.

When we landed, a young corporal came up to me and asked if I was Captain Batavia. I said I was. He said he was sent to pick me up and showed me to a car. I had not seen an automobile, only military type equipment, used in war time.

He said, "Sir, it might be a good idea to put your pistol, rifle and grenades in the trunk."

I had been up north and the only vehicles I had seen were tanks, APC's, and Jeeps. There were no cars, no toilets, nothing but jungle.

As we drove into Saigon there were gas stations, hotels, restaurants, and lots of people. I was put up in a hotel that was for the U.S. military. The next day I was taken to my new duty station, Plantation, a short distance from Saigon. This was where I stayed until my return to the U.S. and departure from the army.

My job was to make sure the men had all kinds of sports available to them when they were out of the jungle and on base. I coordinated competitions between different units and divisions within Vietnam. I also made sure there was lots of equipment available to the men. General Hollingsworth wanted basketball courts, volleyball courts, tennis courts, and plenty of balls for the men's use.

Because the war was coming to an end, the army was releasing me from my "voluntary indefinite" status. It was time for my return to the United States and back to civilian life. As that big, beautiful silver plane lifted off from Vietnam heading home, the men went crazy with excitement, yelling, and clapping; and moments later everyone was sound asleep. After all, this was the first time in a year anyone felt safe from death! I landed at Travis Air Force Base in Fairfield, California, about fifty miles from my home in Oakland. My wife and parents were there to meet the plane. My wife had rented an apartment for us to live in on my return.

CHAPTER XVI

ADJUSTING TO CIVILIAN LIFE

Adjusting to civilian life was not as easy as I had thought it would be. I thought I would take up where I had left off. The year was 1972 and the war was to go on for another three years. The war was very unpopular, and living near Berkeley, California, didn't make my transition any easier. I think the hardest part of going off to fight in a war was that my life as I knew it had come to a stop. Yet, the lives of all of my friends back home had continued to go forward.

The military men returning were not met with any parades or thanks for their service. Just the opposite: the boys returning were treated terribly. Unless you have been thrown into a situation where your survival is the most important thing in your day-to-day life, you cannot understand the emotion that comes with it. When you have seen death daily and learned to live without all the amenities you have been used to all your life, it takes quite a toll on your psyche. I don't think anyone is ever the same after having been to war.

I had a hard time adjusting. Friends I had known most of my life would make negative comments about the war.

Family friends of my dad and mom would say, "Why didn't your dad hire an attorney to get you out of the military?"

These kinds of comments hurt me to the core and made me withdraw. Thinking back now, I like to think these so-called friends had no idea how hurtful these comments were to me. Then again none of them had served in the military or perhaps they would have shown some compassion for what I had been through. Here I was again, the different one from my group of childhood friends. Time had moved forward, but my life had stayed back in limbo, just like when I started elementary school.

Then one day at work, I was having a terrible time. My dad was traveling on vacation.

My uncle said, "I can see something is bothering you."

I told him of the comments that friends of my parents had made during a wedding the previous Saturday regarding serving in Vietnam. I was brought up to respect my elders and not to talk back. But I felt frustration and rage at social events when people would make stupid comments regarding the war. I wanted to take a swing at them. There was one person who was a friend of my dad's, who, whenever he saw me, couldn't help making an off-the-cuff comment.

This was becoming my modus operandi. We would get invited to a social event, I would last a short time when someone would say something to set me off, and instead of striking out, my wife and I would abruptly leave.

My uncle would look at me, and I will never forget until the day I die what he said. "You don't owe these people anything. You don't need to respect any of them."

It was like someone hit a switch and a light went on inside me. I realized at that moment they had to earn my respect. Respect is not something you get just because you are older or hold some high position. The army had beat into us young officers that we must earn our men's respect before they would do anything for us. I had completely forgotten. It was like having an epiphany and it lit a fire in me that I believe helped me move forward and allowed me to accomplish whatever I set my mind to do!

Our family had a business. We sold new and used industrial machinery and scrap metal. I needed a job to support my wife so I asked my uncle and dad for a job. I was offered one with the condition that I would carry my weight and not be a drain on the business. Having me as an employee was the least of their problems. As is typical with most youth, I had all kinds of ideas I wanted to implement. My grandfather had started the business, and both my uncle and dad came into it after World War II. I had worked most of my summers there cleaning machinery and sometimes selling a machine or two.

Now I had the opportunity to sell our inventory. It didn't take me long to build customer relationships. We also were open on Saturdays till 2 p.m. Family businesses are very difficult, to say the least with the personalities involved, and having parents not wanting to make changes to the operation. After all, my dad figured the business had been running fine all these years without my input. I would have knock down, drag out fights with him over my ideas.

The arguing would usually end with my dad and uncle saying: "Are you willing to put up your own money?"

Without hesitation I would reply, "You bet."

Then I would get a comment from them: "Don't be a smart ass!"

There was never a compliment or them saying I might have a good idea. But they were always surprised how effective my ideas were, especially when they increased our profitability.

Our business would be what you would call a mom and pop business. We seldom sold machinery outside of the local bay area. Our gross income had always allowed my grandfather, uncle, and dad to provide for their families very comfortably. I think during their years of ownership, with my cousin Mark and me on the payroll, the biggest year they had brought in around eight-hundred thousand dollars.

It was evident to me if our business was going to provide for all our families, we needed to expand and to reach a larger geographical area. I thought that if I had the use of an airplane, we could expand our business by reaching the central valley of California in an hour instead of a three to four hour drive each way. I was entitled to use my GI bill (for those who served in the military) which would pay for a commercial, instrument and multi-engine license.

The requirements under the GI bill were that you had to get your private license on your own, which was your responsibility financially. This also meant a lot of time back in a classroom setting. The instrument rating especially demanded a lot of classroom instruction in weather and identification of different types of weather patterns and cloud formations. Once again, I struggled to understand all the technical information I had to learn. I went to school two nights a week for four hours. I already had my private pilot's license, so it was assumed all of us students knew how to fly.

Instrument instruction was about 80 percent in the classroom. This was a very difficult challenge for me. At least now I had the knowledge that I could conquer anything I put my mind to. Once again, the reading and comprehension were like a repeat nightmare that never went away. At least I didn't have to write papers to be turned in or read in front of the class. I never thought much about it, but how does a person with learning disabilities fly a complex aircraft, at two-hundred miles an hour or 3.33 miles per minute, and take commands from the traffic control center, switching radio frequencies and direction all at the same time? I taught myself to concentrate and to excel at the task at hand. There is no room for mistakes flying a plane. I knew it would be easy for me to mix up numbers or directions, especially at the rate of speed I would be traveling.

I repeated all commands I received from the air traffic controller, who would say, "Read back correct", or he would repeat the command again.

I would read it back to him, until I heard "read back correct". I found this to be another level of protection, to alleviate any chance of making a mistake. It worked very well for me. It took over a year for me to go through each rating, but soon I held a commercial, multi-engine, and instrument license. Once again, I had proven to myself and those teachers how wrong they were about me.

My next hurdle was going to be convincing my dad and uncle that the plane would be useful as a new tool for our company. My skin must be as thick as a rhinoceros hide. When I brought up the subject of using an airplane in our business, as always, the topic of expense along with getting my dad and uncle to think about trying something new ended with a NO! Then the lecture.

Clyde's Commercial Pilot's License

"We have survived all these years without a plane, and we will keep on surviving without one!" I thought if they were going to continue to be so thickheaded, I would provide the airplane at my own expense.

CHAPTER XVII
THINKING
OUTSIDE THE BOX

I n the beginning, I would rent a plane to either pick up a potential customer and bring him to our warehouse or take a customer to inspect a machine that was hours away by car. Business people don't like spending time traveling to inspect a machine because time is money! When I proposed taking them to see one in an hour by plane instead of hours by car, I got a very positive response. I also think customers liked the idea of flying in a private plane. It had a very prestigious feeling to it. It didn't take long for my dad and uncle to see my sales increase.

I would fly to a city in the central valley, pick up the customer, bring him back to our showroom and get the order on the way back to his city. My dad and uncle, especially my uncle, questioned my ability years before about my being able to carry my weight and not be a drag on the company. It was turning out that they couldn't keep up with my sales. When their accountant pointed out the reason for the increase in our gross income, it didn't take either of them long to ask me if I would fly them somewhere to pick up a potential customer. I eventually

Clyde and his wife, Gail: "Our plane"

bought a used airplane and they were very willing to pay its expenses for business trips.

My sales were better than good and I finally was being compensated for them. One of the first things my wife and I did before our son was old enough to go to school was to move from our first home to a home in an exclusive area called Piedmont. As fate would have it, we purchased it privately from the owners who happened to be family friends. Otherwise, we never could have afforded it. They gave us a good deal and we bought the house.

We had lived in Piedmont for a short time when an issue came up in the city. After World War II the city donated land to the Veterans of Foreign Wars (VFW) and they built a very nice Veterans Memorial Building. The issue at hand was the Piedmont Police Department now wanted to take it over for their own expansion. This was gaining a lot of attention between the city council and veterans.

The membership of the VFW was made up of judges, attorneys, businessmen, and many other affluent people. Apparently, the city felt since it was on their land, they had the right to take over the Veterans Memorial building and leave the veterans without a building of their own. The city and veterans were dug in to fight this out. The mayor of Piedmont wanted to get the veterans to the table to try to negotiate a solution.

The veterans demanded that the arbitrator should be a veteran, while the city demanded the veteran not belong to the VFW. One night, there was knock at my door, and the mayor asked if she could come in and speak to me. Somehow, my name had come up since I was a veteran and I didn't belong to the VFW. She asked me if would consider arbitrating the issue. I said the only way I would consider doing it was that I must have full authority and whatever the outcome, both sides would abide by it. I told the mayor I wanted my demand in writing.

Days later she got back to me and said both sides wanted to interview me before they consented to me arbitrating the issue. I was interviewed separately, without the other side present. Both sides consented to having me arbitrate, and they signed the agreement to abide by my decision.

The arbitration deal was made public, a date was announced, and the meeting would be open to the public. The venue was to be held in the city auditorium. The evening it took place, the auditorium was at full capacity, standing room only. Presentations were made and documents were exchanged by both sides. It was actually a simple fix with each side giving a little and taking less than they wanted.

I really enjoyed being able to solve the issue. After all my time in the military, I was used to going in and fixing problems. I think when you have had learning disabilities to deal with all your life, and have been called names, and have been the last one chosen or left behind, you are more sensitive and feel that no one was ever sensitive towards you. Perhaps these life lessons have given me a different way to see issues.

Having been in the service for nearly three years I never really paid much income tax. Our pay was made up of our weekly amount plus allowances. We didn't pay tax on housing allowances or hazardous duty allowance. Tax was only calculated on what was determined as pay. I was making money now, and when the time came for me to pay income tax, I was not happy about it. I think I disliked paying tax almost as much as I disliked school.

A friend from the old neighborhood, actually Patty's brother Chris, was several years older and I saw him as a mentor. He had served in the navy and become the Secretary of the Port of Oakland. I had a lot of respect for Chris, and we talked often. When I saw how much I was going to pay in taxes I can remember being upset. I called him and he said, "You need to own apartments so you can write them off against taxes."

CHAPTER XVIII
TAKING CHANCES

He set up a lunch with his realtor who had sold him a couple of 4-plexes. That began my introduction to Jack and becoming a landlord. Jack explained that he would show me the ropes of running apartments. He said the golden rule was if I didn't like a property he was showing me, I shouldn't buy it. He said I needed to have an instant "like".

Shortly after our lunch meeting, he called, and I purchased my first four-unit apartment. He showed me how to set up everything. I had to get insurance, accounts with the water company, garbage and power. All these things were learning experiences. I learned how to set up a ledger, fill out rental agreements and all that goes with operating as a landlord. I bought a book put out by Reader's Digest on how to fix the rentals. It explained how to do minor household repairs. I figured if I could get through college, and the army, I could learn from the book and do the repairs myself.

When you own properties, it is not without issues. I did have some evictions in the early years. I had to go to court and present my case to the judge. That meant I had not only to fill out papers for the clerk of the court, but also had to be able to present my case in writing and orally. Of the few eviction cases I had over the forty-eight years I was a landlord, I never lost a case in court. The knowledge and experience I gained in negotiating with the court were invaluable. Everything having to do with legal work also requires being able to read and write. If only the teachers had worked with me those first few years in grammar school, it would have made these obstacles much easier for me.

My tenants, for the most part, were excellent tenants. Because most of the apartments were close to the University of California and the College of Arts and Sciences, many of my tenants were students. They were mostly very responsible. If they weren't, though, a call to their parents carried a tremendous amount of leverage. I had learned in the army to treat men the same way I wanted to be treated. That knowledge paid dividends for me. It didn't take long for my tenants to become part of the neighborhood and to become aware of the goings on around them. As I built a reputation of being a good, decent landlord, I would get an occasional call from a tenant telling me that an owner in the neighborhood was interested in selling his apartment building. The tenant would give me the name and phone number of the person and let me know that if I were to buy it, their friends would rent the units. It didn't take long before I was increasing the number of apartments I owned.

In the beginning I was catching flak from my dad and uncle, as they thought the apartments would take away from the family business. They were also products of the Great Depression. They were calling me a slum lord. My dad went to his attorney, worried that I was buying rental property, and asked what he should do about it. His attorney was an old fraternity brother with a large business clientele in the bay area. He himself owned a fair amount of rental property and told dad he couldn't go wrong owning property. Soon after, my dad was asking if he could be a partner in my next purchase. I said, "Sure!" It wasn't long before I owned property with my dad, brother and sister. Who would have thought the one with learning issues was making everyone wealthy!

The industry we were in had an association called the Machinery Dealers National Association (MDNA). The two-story office building was located, at that time, in Silver Springs, Maryland. The overwhelming concentration of used machinery dealers was in the midwest and east coast of the United States. There were also many chapters all over the United States, Europe, South Africa, and Canada. The majority of companies like ours were located in the Los Angeles area of Southern California, whereas Northern California was known for light industry. The association was always looking for new members.

A young guy named Mark, whose family business was like ours but located in Los Angeles, kept trying to get me to go to a chapter meeting. Eventually when I was on business one day in Los Angeles, I stuck around in the evening to attend the meeting. I was quite impressed seeing many machinery dealers sharing information together, and I learned that some of them co-owned machines. I remembered thinking that was a good way to expand our business from just being local. I talked to my dad and uncle and asked why we didn't belong to the MDNA. My dad kept saying all they did was play craps in the back room after the meetings. He definitely did not see how it was going to help our business and could only see it as another expense. I kept working on my uncle and dad, and they eventually let me attend more chapter meetings.

Every year around May, the MDNA held a convention. Though the machinery industry was small compared to the automobile or steel industry, the conventions were definitely five star all the way. The first year my dad and uncle decided to attend, the convention was in Las Vegas. I think going to Las Vegas was the driving factor to get them to go. They decided that my dad and I would go first, while my uncle and his son would go the next year. We would leapfrog years. I think my dad came away from the convention with a different perspective about MDNA.

There were lectures on issues that pertained to our type of business and speakers from Washington D.C. There were about four-hundred machinery dealers in attendance. It was an opportunity to meet owners of similar businesses from all over the United States as well as the world. It was also an opportunity to share business ideas and learn how others operated their businesses.

After dad and I attended the convention, there was less resistance about me flying down to Los Angeles to attend chapter meetings. During the year, the MDNA put on seminars and programs and introduced new office products on the market to help all of us operate our companies more efficiently. Our industry, though small comparatively to the auto, steel, or oil industry, was important to the global economy. If manufacturers worldwide were purchasing machinery, that meant companies large and small were busy and expanding. It also meant unemployment was down and the economy was good. At that time there was no hi tech, cell phones, or Wi-Fi.

I had a hard-charging, rough way about me wanting to accomplish certain things in our industry when I was told they couldn't be done. I am not one you can say "can't do" to. I had heard that all my life from teachers and at the university. By this time in my life, though, I realized there was nothing I couldn't do. Apparently, I had impressed the officers and committee chairmen who were running the MDNA.

One day my dad and uncle received a call from the nominating committee chairman who at one time had been president of MDNA. There was a director-at-large position open that had not been filled. He wanted to offer it to me. Initially my dad was against it, but my uncle thought it might be good for our business image. They called my cousin Mark and me into their office where a vote was held. Being on the board would mean time away from the business plus the cost of airline tickets and hotels, as meetings and seminars were held all over the U. S. My dad and uncle called Harvey in Tennessee and said they would allow me to serve one year.

The year was 1978, and this was the beginning of a new chapter in my life that turned out to play a big role. By 1991 I had gone up the ladder from committee chairman to president of MDNA. I am to this date the only person west of the Colorado River to ever hold the position of president.

CHAPTER XIX
BECOMING PRESIDENT

During October 1985, Mark and I purchased the business from our fathers and in 1991, I became president of the MDNA. As president I also held a seat on the Association of European Machine Tool Merchants Board (AEMTM). The MDNA had always been run by midwest and east coast machinery dealers. The MDNA was a conglomerate and parent company that oversaw its subsidiaries, the Machinery Information System (MIS) which was a publication company; the Association of Machinery Equipment Appraisers (AMEA) and the scholarship foundation.

The presidents of all the subsidiaries reported to me. I oversaw their agendas, finances and operations as well. Here was my name at the top of the organization table. Me, the student who would never amount to anything, now running a conglomerate. I only wish those teachers could have seen me now.

Being president of MDNA opened many doors, opportunities and experiences for the kid who wasn't destined to achieve anything in life. During that time, I was called to Washington D.C. for meetings with different heads of state and department heads. It turns out the MDNA was the only association in the U.S. whose business interest was used equipment. When the State

Department was being asked by foreign countries for used medical equipment, they had no idea where to go until they realized there was an association in the U.S. that dealt with used equipment. Even though it wasn't medical equipment, it was still used industrial equipment. I was asked to go to Washington, D.C. and meet with the Secretary of State.

I met with the Deputy Secretary and explained our industry did not sell used medical equipment, but what an experience for me! On another occasion I met with the Deputy Secretary of the Treasury. It had come to the department's attention that used machinery was bringing more money into today's market than it did when originally purchased and they thought there was an opportunity to put a tax on used machinery. I spent several days there in meetings. When I finally left, they decided it would be too cumbersome to know which machines appreciated and which did not.

The Federal Reserve was also looking into the appreciation and depreciation of machine tools, and once again I was off to Washington. I was introduced to Alan Greenspan, who was head of the Federal Reserve at that time. I was credited with contributing to and helping with writing the report on appreciation of machinery.

One of the biggest issues that still faces people in the new and used machine tool sales today is product liability. Every state has a different law as it pertains to the statute of limitations. California has no statute of limitations. This means a person injured on a machine sold by a dealer, even though it was manufactured in 1920, can still sue. Every state seems to have a different statute of limitations. Nevada's is two years. This is a huge issue for machinery dealers. Legal action can be taken depending on the years of statute limitation.

MDNA and other industries had been lobbying for years for a uniform product liability legislation bill. This would guarantee that all states would have the same statute of limitations. I received an invitation to meet with the President of the United States, George H. Bush, at the White House. Thirty-five of us had been asked to meet with him to discuss product liability. That was very impressive and exciting for me. After all, even my parents didn't know anyone who had been a guest of a president in the White House.

Prior to my visit to the White House I had to be cleared by Security. They requested certain types of identification which I sent on. I had borrowed my dad's cashmere overcoat as it was either February or March, and overcoats were worn back there. I showed up an hour early and walked up to the door, where a military person was stationed. He asked my name and purpose and wanted to see a photo ID. He talked into his sleeve, where a microphone was hidden. Then he opened the door for me, and a female Air Force officer asked for my overcoat. She handed me what looked like a casino chip with the presidential emblem in the middle, and with a number for reclaiming my coat when I left. I was told the meeting would be held in the Blue Room in approximately one hour.

I was free to wander around but was asked not to go upstairs where the President's personal quarters were. I thought, "Boy, if the old gang could see me now wandering around the White House!" I went into the dining room, kitchen, theater, and all the rooms where I was permitted to roam. Even the bathrooms had the presidential emblem on the toilet paper and the folded paper towels. I stuffed a couple of those paper towels in my pocket, which I still have in a scrap book. Then that old devil in me surfaced. Me, being me, thought how great it would it be to say I took a poop in the White House and so I did. This was from the boy sitting in the corner of the cloak room on a red chair to sitting on the porcelain throne as a guest in the White House. Even I was in awe of my surroundings. This was like the cherry on top of the whipped cream...and it didn't stop there!

A few months later there was a gala function to be held at the Kennedy Center for the Queen of England. Broadway actors from New York were going to put on "Phantom of the Opera". Our association received an invitation. My wife didn't want to go because the kids were young, but I wasn't going to miss this black-tie opportunity. The Queen of England was sitting in the presidential box with the President. The Kennedy Center was packed with senators, congressmen and heads of state. At intermission champagne and finger food goodies were served. It was something I will never forget. Here I was the boy in the corner rubbing shoulders with these influential people in this beautiful venue at the Kennedy Center.

My mother always told me that I would get something out of whatever I was willing to put into it. How true. I gave everything I had to the MDNA. I rose up the ladder at a time the association was having trouble getting young people to step up. Nepotism was fairly normal in our type of business. Family businesses are difficult at best, having to work with parents, brothers and sisters with our different personalities and sometimes at odds with each other.

When the association approached my dad and uncle seeking approval to offer me a seat as a director-at-large, the MDNA was in decline. Chapters were losing membership, as the association had become stale with no new blood to resurrect it. I came along, a West Coast ass-kicking army guy who was making a lot of noise wanting to know why the association wasn't accomplishing any of its goals. I was told years later that they took a big gamble on me.

First of all, midwest and east coast people have a different outlook on the way things are done. Easterners seem to be much more polite, whereas I was more like a Patton. In fact, my first vice-president would call me George as in George Patton.

When I became second vice-president and through my presidential term, I traveled at my company's expense to every chapter and went to meetings all over the U. S. I fell back on my military education to lead by example which was exactly what I did. I found that the chapters really enjoyed seeing the president of the MDNA. The receptions I attended from the different chapters were amazing. They put on dinners and events in my honor. This was different from my philosophy of prior years, where I wasn't polished and believed if I wanted to make tiger soup, I had to go and get the tiger! I had always been told I was a bull in china shop! During my last year as president, a travel fund for future presidents was created specifically for them to visit all the chapters.

It didn't take long for the chapters to start gaining membership. Suddenly, the next generation was taking an interest in MDNA. I was making it fun and I kept the association off balance. Members wanted to be a part of this association with the crazy guy from the West Coast. One time I had our executive director put on the agenda a proposal I got from an aircraft company to purchase a jet aircraft so I could travel to the different chapters. I had it put in the board book.

The board book was sent to all directors prior to the actual board meetings. I wanted to see who was reading the material before we had our board of director's meeting. There were twenty-seven directors from all over the U. S. and Europe, South Africa, and Canada. I learned very quickly that they had read the material prior to the meeting. What an uproar it caused when they thought I really wanted a jet aircraft. We had some great laughs. I liked keeping everyone on their toes, and it created a positive interest in what was going on within the association.

I had two excellent guys a little younger than myself, step up and suddenly the association had new life with a bright group to run it for years to come. The industry in the 1970's was run predominantly by men. Some of the businesses were husband and wife teams. I saw great potential in one such woman. I conferred with my first vice-president to get his opinion about bringing her name up before the nominating committee be an officer. The nominating committee was made up of the older guys who had served as president. We called them the "old gray hairs". John, my first vice-president, thought it a good idea and agreed. When I finished my term and became the immediate past president, she moved up to second vice-president. She became the first woman to be an officer in the MDNA and eventually became its president.

I have always heard CEO's, owners and presidents of large companies say, "If you want to take advantage of your competition, get them on a board of directors". I couldn't disagree more. It took a lot of time away from my company, and it was costly. In my case it made me recognizable and popular worldwide and opened doors for our company. I was invited to participate in a partnership in purchasing equipment in Asia and Europe. I learned how to get an agent overseas by contacting the Federal Reserve, where I had done some work. I learned how to do bills of lading, letters of credit, set up shipping via ocean going ships, and to open top containers versus regular containers as machinery can be too tall to put in a regular container.

For me, all the reading and filling out of forms was tedious work. I had to concentrate and make sure all paperwork was done correctly. This meant for me reading and re-reading to make sure I had not made a mistake. The more I did it the better I got at it. We used what is called an" irrevocable letter of credit", which meant the seller didn't get paid until the ship pulled away from the pier. We would have containers on the water every month. We were now becoming very well known in Japan, and I was asked to speak to a group of Japanese machinery dealers in Nagoya. This was a new experience, as they had an interpreter stand next to me at the podium. I would say a sentence, then she would say that sentence in Japanese. I was also the only "round eye" there. They nicknamed me Shogun.

Japan and Europe were saturated with businessmen buying and selling equipment and shipping it back to the United States. I was traveling back and forth to Asia, sometimes several times in one month. I flew first class which gave me entrance to the first-class lounge. Those of us who travel internationally on business start seeing the same people in the lounges. I got to know a few of the people who worked for some major companies from all over the U. S. To kill the time before our flights we would all discuss what we were doing or trying to accomplish.

Clyde D. Batavia

CHAPTER XX
GOING INTERNATIONAL

One day a couple of the guys said, "You really ought to be looking for an agent in Malaysia where there's less competition". It made sense to me, but I had no idea how to go about getting an agent in a foreign country. Then one day my secretary buzzed me and said there were two gentlemen from the State Department to see me. They said that I had inquired about seeking an agent in Malaysia but was too late for that country. However, Vietnam was beginning to open up, and President Clinton was hoping to start a diplomatic relationship with Vietnam. I immediately stated, and not in a soft tone, that I had gotten out of there with my life, and I had no intention of ever going back. They said they would send me the weekly intelligence on Vietnam in case I changed my mind. My wife suggested I return to Vietnam, hoping that even if I didn't do any business there, it would help me get over the stigma of war.

Some months later I called the State Department in San Francisco and said I would like to meet with them again. We met, and after a question and answer period, I finally consented to go. They also informed me that the United States had no diplomatic relations with Vietnam at that point and that I would have to go through a Chinese company in San Diego that they had selected.

I was contacted by a Mr. Lee, who interviewed me and wanted to know what our company wished to accomplish. I was told they would have to get me a visa. When I disclosed that I had been a captain in Vietnam during the war, a perplexed look came over Mr. Lee's face. He said they would have to review any potential problems and get back to me. When he contacted me again, he informed me that the Vietnamese government required that I disclose everywhere I had been while I was "in country" during the war. I put a list together, to the best of my memory, of places I had been and forwarded it to Mr. Lee.

A few months later, he contacted me and said he had gotten me a visa and had made me reservations at a hotel in Saigon for my stay. To me it will always be Saigon, but the correct name today is Ho Chi Minh City. Mr. Lee had also made reservations for me at the Hotel Hanoi where I would be staying during the second part of my trip.

I was told when I arrived in Vietnam to make my way to the hotel. The next day an agent from the government met me and took me around the city to introduce me to companies. About a week before I left on this adventure, representatives from the State Department out of San Francisco showed up at my office. They handed me a brown envelope containing some clean syringes and two maps. The maps showed the locations of the Swiss and French Embassies. I questioned why I needed them and was told it was insurance just in case I were to run into a problem. If that should happen, the Swiss or French embassy would take me in and give me safe haven. The syringes were in case I contracted cholera or required an injection. I was told the country had serums and vaccines but might not have clean syringes.

I was getting that queasy feeling in the pit of my stomach, about going back to a place I was lucky enough to get out of alive! Otherwise, everything had sounded good to me. Then I learned flying into Vietnam was not so easy. Because the U. S. had no diplomatic relations, there were no U. S. airlines that could fly into Saigon. I ended up flying to Hong Kong. From there only two airlines flew into Vietnam: Vietnam Air or Air France. Vietnam Air was being subsidized by Thai Airlines. I chose Air France. It was one in the morning when my plane landed in Vietnam.

It was not an airport as you know it but was the old Tan Son Nhut Air Force Base left behind by the U.S.

Clyde's return to former Tan Son Nahat Air Force Base,
in 1995, Tan Son Nahat International Airport

Military. As the plane taxied, I recognized the airfield from years before, and chills ran down my back. I was wondering what in the hell I was doing back here. Customs and Immigration were done out on the tarmac since there was no real terminal. Instead, there was a large chain link fence to separate the passengers from the Vietnamese people on the other side. There were crowds of people yelling at us passengers, wanting to sell us things or give us a ride into town.

The airport was quite a long drive to the center of the city. I somehow made my way to the hotel with the directions Mr. Lee had given me that were written in Vietnamese. To my surprise the hotel was very clean and much nicer than I had expected. I had the next day off before I was to meet the agent. I started walking down the street, and soon a man approached me and asked what I was doing in Vietnam. He was one of two other Americans on the flight from Hong Kong the night before. Everyone else on the flight had been Asian. I told him I was there to look for possible business opportunities.

He asked if I had served during the Vietnam War and I responded that I had. He also had been in-country

during the war. He asked me to wait until he returned with two other gentlemen. They explained that one of them had been a war correspondent in the early 1960's before the war escalated. He was now the anchor for ABC New York local news. He had come back for the twentieth anniversary of the fall of Saigon. At that time, I think we were the only four Americans in Vietnam. There were no others to be seen anywhere. He said this would make a good story: "Serviceman returns looking for business opportunities". I said I was interested and got into their van with them. We drove to a major city intersection. They ran a mic up my shirt, and the anchor did an interview that was aired in New York. He also sent me a copy of what had aired.

The following morning, I met my representative, a woman dressed in a black Aodai, the traditional wear for women. She had a government car and took me around, introducing me to people in charge of companies that might be a good fit for our company and could serve as an agent for us. After a week in Saigon, I made my way to the airport and headed north to Hanoi. This was an in-country flight on Air Vietnam in an old Boeing 727. I was the only American on board. There were two Swiss gentlemen who were in the business of leasing aircraft. After a harrowing flight that was supposed to take several hours but turned into ten due to weather issues, we landed in Hanoi.

There were no taxis or buses, and the city and hotel were about an hour away. In the pitch dark I stood with some Vietnamese people. No one spoke English. A van pulled up and they crammed into it like sardines. I kept saying, "Hanoi, Hanoi?" Then they waved me over and gestured that I was to get into the van. It was that or nothing. I figured I would take a chance with these

Vietnamese. I was exhausted and put my faith in my assumption that I would be okay. They had chickens in bamboo cages tied on top of the van. Inside, people were sitting on each other. Eventually we made it to the city, and I climbed over the other passengers to exit. Not able to speak their language, I bowed toward them and they bowed back.

I finally checked into a hotel built by the Russians when they had been in Vietnam. Rooms were very stark, dark, and basic. I was escorted to my room. A woman sat in a chair directly outside it all night. I believe to this day that my room was bugged. After a couple of hours of sleep, I met my representative and off we went to find a suitable person to represent our company. After spending several days in Hanoi, I headed back to the good old USA, happy to be on my way home alive and well.

This had been the first of many trips for me that would follow. It turned out to be just what I needed to help me get over my war-time experience in Vietnam. Everyone I had met had been very warm and helpful. The only signs of the American Army having fought in the country were the museums and monuments. Those were difficult to visit as they held all kinds of equipment that had been left or captured during the war and pictures of dead Americans. As they say, "The victors get to write the history".

Chapter XXI
Return to Vietnam

I am not so sure we would have been as forgiving as the Vietnamese people seemed to be. Vietnam was a poor country, and at the minimum, a third world country. The war had taken a big toll on whatever economy they might have had prior to it. The country definitely needed industrial machinery to help rebuild its infrastructure.

I had been introduced to a gentleman, Mr. Gioc, while in Saigon, who was the head of a company called Mecanimex. He seemed to be the best prospect as an agent for our company, and he spoke excellent English.

Once back in Oakland, I started investigating how to do business in Vietnam. Many factors had to be dealt with. After all, in the machinery world among other things, you need to be able to ship heavy equipment and know how to get paid. My first call was to Chris, since he was the Secretary of the Port of Oakland. I learned since we had no diplomatic relationship with Vietnam, we could not ship to it directly. The shipments would have to go to Hong Kong to be unloaded and re-loaded onto another ship that could legally sail to Vietnam. Then there was the issue of the shallow entrance to the harbor in Vietnam, which required a ship loaded with equipment that didn't draft a lot of water.

Chris told me to contact a company in Oakland called Indo-China Express. The owner of the company turned out to be very knowledgeable. I told him of my adventure in Vietnam and that I was thinking of asking Mr. Gioc to act as an agent for our company. He told me he had been doing business with Mr. Gioc for a while and that he was very honorable. He also said that Mr. Gioc had contacted him to check me out. He filled me in on who Mr. Gioc was. He was high up in the Vietnamese government, in charge of importing and exporting equipment and all goods into Vietnam. That was the beginning of my relationship with Mr. Gioc.

After a few more of my trips to Vietnam, we came to an agreement. His company would provide us with a showroom in Hanoi and would also run it. We would send them the machinery at our expense, and they would pay us as they sold the machines. Mark and I decided to take a chance. We conferred as to what types of machines they felt would sell. We shook hands and they kept their promise as we did ours. It became a successful experience. No letter of credit was required, as is the usual way to do business internationally, just the honor and handshake of two men whose countries were once at war with each other.

Then the request came from Mr. Gioc to help him put on an international tool show. He was asking me for my advice. I had never done anything like this, but after doing some research, I told him who I thought should be contacted. It was a small machinery show, but it was their first. My wife and I were guests of the Vietnamese government for a week. The show was held in Ho Chi Minh City. Not long after that I heard from Mr. Gioc, who requested a meeting with me in Hanoi. He said some of the heads of state would be in attendance, and that they wanted to discuss a proposal with me. I flew back to Hanoi and the meeting was held at his home around the dining table...a most unusual meeting place.   There were three or four gentleman I was introduced to, who were in charge of everything from energy, commerce, finances, and customs.... all major components to run a country. Another very distinguished gentleman at the table was a Mr. Fong, whom I had met before with Mr. Gioc. He was a tall man with white hair, who always wore black turtleneck sweaters with black blazers and pants and sat at the table very quietly. The men discussed the importance of purchasing good machinery and equipment for Vietnam to grow and develop as a country and to help build good infrastructure.

They wanted me to supply them with all kinds of machinery and manuals for the machinery. They were offering to do what is called a BBT (Buy Build and Transfer). The government would build a facility we needed, and we would fill it with machinery and manuals. I would be responsible for training the Vietnamese and overseeing the operation. After we had made a certain profit, which was to be agreed upon by both parties over a five-year period, we would transfer the entire operation over to the Vietnamese.

During our conversations at Mr. Gioc's home, Mr. Fong pulled a photo out and slid it across the table. It was a picture of himself and a couple of the other gentleman sitting at the table in front of the Eiffel Tower in Paris with Henry Kissinger. The people I was sitting with were part of the Paris Peace Talks, which ended the Vietnam war. I now realized just how high up in the government these men were who I was dealing with. These were the same men who were going to shape and mold the new Vietnam. I said I would investigate their proposal and that

I would need to contact other dealers in Europe and leasing companies who might be interested in the feasibility of financing a deal of this magnitude. I told them I would get back to them when I had more information.

Having been the president of the MDNA and sitting on the EATMM board, I thought if anyone could put this together, I could. It was very exciting. I saw it as the greatest thing I would ever accomplish. I started making calls and before long I had commitments from the European group to supply the machinery. I committed to supplying the manuals with the help of other dealers who had gone into the manual business. I contacted JLC (Japanese Lease Corporation) using my contacts in Japan.

JLC was one of the biggest in the world at that time and committed to doing all the financing. I then contacted people in Washington, D. C. I had met to make sure I wasn't going to violate any international laws. I learned there was all kinds of paperwork that needed to be filled out and fees for permits when doing business with foreign countries. My least favorite thing was having to read all the U. S. section codes, rules and laws pertaining to doing business in a foreign country. The print on government paper is very small, and that didn't help with my reading and comprehending section codes and government regulations. It seemed like it took me an eternity to understand all of it, especially when some of the words had legal meanings. I trudged through the U. S. foreign codes, and when I thought I understood what I read, I made an application. The team of dealers and finance people I had put together were excited to be on board.

My next step was to set up a meeting with all the respective parties in Ho Chi Minh City. The date was made, and everyone was looking forward to getting together. After all, this was the opening of a new country for business. My excitement wasn't because of the idea of making money; it was that I, the kid who spent most of his grammar school years in the corner of the cloak room, who was told over and over that I was going nowhere in life, was actually putting this international coalition together.

CHAPTER XXII
UNDEFEATED

I t had been decided by the Vietnamese that they wanted me to oversee the operation. But don't count your chickens before they hatch! One month before we were all to meet in Ho Chi Minh City, the Japanese economy suffered a major collapse. This caused a huge impact, especially all over Asia. Shortly thereafter I received a fax from Mr. Gioc in Vietnam suggesting we call off the meeting until the Asian economy rebounded. As it turned out, circumstances beyond my control killed the whole deal. I had come so close, but the exercise itself was rewarding to me and I knew in my own mind that I was capable of such a feat.

I finished my term as president of MDNA in 1992 but remained on the board in positions customarily held by past presidents till 1997. I felt I had done all I could for the enhancement of MDNA, and it was time for me to move on. I was still traveling all over the world buying machinery. It was around 1998 into 1999 that I was seeing a slowdown in the U.S. economy. Machines that had been hard to purchase on the international used market were suddenly becoming more available. By end of 1999 there was a glut of the highly sought-after machines. Typically, when I would purchase a machine overseas it would be sold before it hit the shores of the U.S. But things were changing. Asia was slowing down, which was part of the reason for more machines on the market. The other reason was due to low interest rates in Japan; the turnover rate for manufacturers was much faster than in the U.S.

I was getting nervous observing the slowdown and fearful it would end up in the U.S. Boy, was my insight right on the mark. I could see the writing on the wall. I might be a lousy reader of books, but this had been easy for me to comprehend. I discussed the situation with my cousin Mark. We agreed the cleanest, quickest way to get out of the machinery business before it collapsed was to auction it off and rent out our buildings. That is exactly what we did. We got enough from our auction to pay off the credit line with our bank. Then we rented out our buildings. It turned out we made more money from renting them than from running our business.

In 1999 my wife and I decided that we would like to spend more time at Lake Tahoe. We had our 1922 cabin torn down and rebuilt. In April of 2000 we moved into our rustic rebuilt cabin. The changing economy, the decision to auction off the assets of the business and our renting of the buildings had me re-examining my financial position. I had been so busy working and building up our business that I had not realized I had amassed enough financial stability to retire. I still had the rental properties to operate but felt that would keep me busy enough. Soon we found we were spending more time and enjoying our retirement in Tahoe. We sold our house in Piedmont and purchased a small house in Alameda, where we stayed when visiting our parents. Lake Tahoe became our full-time residence until 2018, when we purchased a home in Reno but kept the Tahoe cabin.

When we moved up to Tahoe in 2000, I had promised my wife that I would not get involved with being on any more boards or being a director on a board, as I had served on many of them and also had been involved in civic issues during our marriage. Unfortunately, this promise was short-lived as I got pulled into being on the board of our HOA (Homeowners Association). I ended up becoming the president of the association for close to fifteen years.

They say your reputation follows you. The more we got involved in the Tahoe community, the more people got to know us. I was asked to be an adviser on the Gene Upshaw Golf Tournament in Truckee, California. Proceeds from the tournament went to helping people pay for medical things not covered by insurance and for research of medical devices to help keep rural medical care low. The cancer center at Tahoe Forest Hospital in Truckee, under construction and soon to open, was named after Gene Upshaw.

My experience was very positive. We received support from many major corporations, including the NFL Players Association, the Raiders football team, and many well-known athletes.

After a couple of years on that advisory board, I was asked to sit on the Tahoe Institute Rural Health Research (TIRHR) Board. This was a board under the umbrella of the hospital board, whose purpose was to find medical devices that would help cut costs for rural health care. Tahoe Forest Hospital is the only rural hospital connected to the University of California Medical Center. One of the requirements to be in partnership with the University of California, San Francisco Medical School, is to do research. I am still sitting on that board today, but I don't plan on serving on any more boards at age 74. I think I have done my fair share!

"A ride on the wild side" was the term my father used to describe raising me at a roast my wife gave me for my fiftieth birthday. All I ever heard from teachers and even the university was that I would never amount to anything nor succeed at whatever I tried. Instead of helping and teaching me, my educators left me behind to become someone who would not be able to meet any of life's challenges. It is easier to teach kids who have no learning issues, but it takes a "real" teacher to teach those who learn differently. As you have read, I still managed to accomplish many things over the years.

My mother, all five feet and ninety-five pounds, never gave up on me; nor would she let me give up on myself. She took on the schools and teachers with the ferocity of a grizzly bear. Worst of all, in my mind at the time, she took me on! She was tireless and tenacious! Sometimes I would spend a weekend in my room with her, going page by page, sentence by sentence until I understood what I was reading. Most of the time, though, it was my will against hers. Fortunately, she always prevailed.

One Friday afternoon, my English teacher at the high school called mom for a meeting. When mom came home, she asked me if I was prepared for Monday's test on Julius Caesar. I probably said I would study for it during the weekend. That weekend was spent in my bedroom. It was my will against hers. It was no contest. She won as usual. By the end of the weekend I could recite Julius Caesar forwards and backwards and even learned to enjoy the story line. To this day, I can recite most of Julius Caesar by memory. When the test results came back, the teacher accused me of cheating. In front of the entire class, he said there was no way I could have gotten an A without cheating.

When my mom asked how I did on the test, I explained what the teacher had said in front of the class. The next day my English teacher and the high school principal felt the wrath of my mom and I did receive an apology. It was a constant fight for me, always being put down by people who had been put on a pedestal. After all, I was always told to listen to my teachers. They were the educators; they were the smartest people. You may understand now why even today I still have those same negative feelings.

Looking back over my seventy-four years, it's been quite a ride! I was a child with learning disabilities and dyslexia in a time when no one knew how to deal with learning disabilities. The great and mighty know-it-all educators hadn't had a solution to help me learn. I didn't fit their mold, so I was left to fend for myself. My scars will never go away because I missed out on all the basic learning skills taught in those early years in grammar school. That is where students' core base of learning begins. Students build on that base for the rest of their formal education. If you are deficient in these skills, it creates difficulties for everyday living, such as reading, writing and math. I can't emphasize enough how important having that base is to build on for the rest of your life.

I am not quite sure I know how I was able to accomplish so many things, how I rose to lead so many different organizations and become financially comfortable. Today I would have been diagnosed with ADHD (Attention Deficit/Hyperactivity Disorder), dyslexia, and processing disorder. There can be no doubt that had my mother listened to the teachers in my various schools, I would have turned out to be a different person.

Instead, she fought for me, and in so doing, taught me to fight for myself. After all, I am one of those who learns by watching. When the educators suggested to my parents to put me in a private school, mom dug her heels in deeper. After all I was her first born, and mothers always think their kids are the most beautiful and smartest ever born.

I think my many accomplishments are due to my never giving up, regardless of how hard something might be. If you keep working at it, you can achieve your goal. If you can't succeed going after a goal the traditional way, then you have to be creative to find another way to reach it. I don't believe there is any one way to teach us how to find our way to improvise or compensate. We have to find it ourselves.

I think if you learn anything from my book it is to do whatever you must to succeed, even if it's different from the usual or traditional way of doing things. That will be the key to your success. Your goal is to accomplish the mission. You may not do it the way others do, but that's not as important as long as you succeed. It makes no difference whether you're learning to fly a plane or becoming the president of a company or organization. There is no obstacle you can't overcome if you just keep focused and don't give up.

ABOUT THE AUTHOR
CLYDE D. BATAVIA, CEA

C lyde D. Batavia was born in Oakland California in 1946. It was a time when educators did not recognize learning disabilities or how to deal with them. Yet without any professional help, the author learned to compensate and succeed at almost everything he has attempted in his life, both in sports and the business world.

Batavia has been in the business of buying and selling new and used machinery since 1972. He has extensive experience as an expert witness and has been successful in the courts and depositions.

Until retiring, Clyde was a member in good standing of the Association of Machinery and Equipment Appraisers (AMEA) and is a Level H Certified Equipment Appraiser. He was a candidate-member of the American Society of Appraisers (ASA) and held membership in the North American Association of Equipment Appraisers, Certified Senior Appraiser level.

Clyde co-authored a paper on machinery depreciation for the Federal Reserve called "Evidence on the Retirement and Depreciation of Machine Tools". He has consulted for the U.S. Treasury Department concerning taxation on aging capital assets. Clyde has been involved in discussions regarding Product Liability Reform with former President Bush at the White House.

In 1991, Clyde was elected for two terms as President of the Machinery Dealers National Association (MDNA) in Washington D.C. He was the first and, still remains to this date, the only machinery dealer to hold the position of President "west of the Mississippi" since the beginning of MDNA in 1942. Clyde was also active in the European Association of Machine Tool Merchants (EAMTM).

Batavia has been a guest speaker all over the country on Products Liability legislation. He presently sits on the board of Tahoe Institute of Rural Health Research at Tahoe Forest Hospital.